PHYSICS

The People Behind the Science

KATHERINE CULLEN, PH.D.

CHELSEA HOUSE
PUBLISHERS
An imprint of Infobase Publishing

Physics: The People Behind the Science

Chelsea House
An imprint of Infobase Publishing
132 West 31st Street
New York NY 10001

Library of Congress Cataloging-in-Publication Data

Cullen, Katherine E.
    Physics: the people behind the science / Katherine Cullen.
        p. cm.—(Pioneers in science)
    Includes bibliographical references and index.
    ISBN 0-8160-5463-0 (hardcover: acid-free paper)
    1. Physicists—Biography. 2. Physics—History. I. Title. II. Series.
    QC15.C85 2005
    530'.092'2—dc222004030238

Chelsea House books are available at special discounts when purchased in bulk quantities for businesses, associations, institutions, or sales promotions. Please call our Special Sales Department in New York at (212) 967-8800 or (800) 322-8755.

You can find Chelsea House on the World Wide Web at
http://www.chelseahouse.com

Text design and composition by Mary Susan Ryan-Flynn
Cover design by Cathy Rincon
Illustrations by Bobbi McCutcheon
Cover printed by Yurchak Printing, Landisville, Pa.
Book printed and bound by Yurchak Printing, Landisville, Pa.

Printed in the United States of America

This book is printed on acid-free paper.

*I dedicate this book to
all future pioneers in science.*

CONTENTS

PREFACE

Being first in line earns a devoted fan the best seat in the stadium. The first runner to break the ribbon spanning the finish line receives a gold medal. The firstborn child inherits the royal throne. Certain advantages or privileges often accompany being the first, but sometimes the price paid is considerable. Neil Armstrong, the first man to walk on the Moon, began flying lessons at age 16, toiled at numerous jobs to pay tuition, studied diligently to earn his bachelor's degree in aerospace engineering, flew 78 combat missions in Korea as a brave navy pilot, worked as a civilian test pilot for seven years, then as an astronaut for NASA for another seven years, and made several dangerous trips into space before the historic *Apollo 11* mission. He endured rigorous physical and mental preparation, underwent years of training, and risked his life to courageously step foot where no man had ever walked before. Armstrong was a pioneer of space exploration; he opened up the way for others to follow. Not all pioneering activities may be as perilous as space exploration. But like the ardent fan, a pioneer in science must be dedicated; like the competitive runner, she must be committed; and like being born to royalty, sometimes providence plays a role.

Science encompasses all knowledge based on general truths or observed facts. More narrowly defined, science refers to a branch of knowledge that specifically deals with the natural world and its laws. Philosophically described, science is an endeavor, a search for truth, a way of knowing, or a means of discovering. Scientists gain information through employing a procedure called the scientific method. The scientific method requires one to state the problem and formulate a testable hypothesis or educated guess to describe a phenomenon or explain an observation, test the hypothesis experimentally or by collecting data from observations, and draw conclusions from the results. Data can eliminate a hypothesis, but never confirm it with absolute certainty; scientists may accept a hypothesis as true when sufficient supporting evidence has been obtained. The process sounds entirely straightforward, but sometimes advancements in science do not follow such a logical approach. Because humans make the observations, generate the hypothesis, carry out the experiments, and draw the conclusions, students of science must recognize the personal dimension of science.

Pioneers in Science is a set of volumes that profile the people behind the science, individuals who initiated new lines of thought or research. They risked possible failure and often faced opposition but persisted to pave new pathways of scientific exploration. Their backgrounds vary tremendously; some never graduated from secondary school, while others earned multiple advanced degrees. Familial affluence allowed some to pursue research unhindered by financial concerns, but others were so poor they suffered from malnutrition or became homeless. Personalities ranged from exuberant to somber and gentle to stubborn, but they all sacrificed, giving their time, insight, and commitment because they believed in the pursuit of knowledge. The desire to understand kept them going when they faced difficulties, and their contributions moved science forward.

The set consists of eight volumes: *Biology, Chemistry, Earth Science, Marine Science, Physics, STS (Science, Technology, and Society), Space and Astronomy,* and *Weather and Climate.* Each book contains 10 biographical sketches of pioneering individuals in a subject, including information about their childhood, how they entered into their scientific careers, their research, and enough background science information for the reader to appreciate their discoveries and contributions. Though all the profiled individuals are certainly distinguished, their inclusion is not intended to imply that they are the greatest scientists of all time. Rather, the profiled individuals were selected to reflect a variety of subdisciplines in each field, different histories, alternative approaches to science, and diverse characters. Each chapter includes a chronology and a list of specific references about the individual and his work. Each book also includes an introduction to the field of science to which its pioneers contributed, line illustrations, photographs, a glossary of scientific terms related to the research described in the text, and a listing of further resources for information about the general subject matter.

The goal of this set is to provide, at an appropriate level, factual information about pioneering scientists. The author hopes that readers will be inspired to achieve greatness themselves, to feel connected to the people behind science, and to believe that they may have a positive and enduring impact on society.

ACKNOWLEDGMENTS

I would like to thank Frank K. Darmstadt, Executive Editor of science and mathematics at Infobase Publishing, for his skillful guidance and extreme patience, and to Melissa Cullen-DuPont, for having all the answers. Appreciation is also extended to illustrator Bobbi McCutcheon for her dedicated professionalism and to Ann E. Hicks and Amy L. Conver for thier constructive suggestions. The reference librarians and support staff of the main branch of the Medina County District Library, located in Medina, Ohio, deserve acknowledgment for their assistance in obtaining interlibrary loans, acquiring numerous special requests, and handling the hundreds of materials and resources the author borrowed during the writing of this set. Gratitude is also expressed to Pam Shirk, former media specialist at A. I. Root Middle School in Medina, Ohio, for sharing her expertise. Many people and organizations generously gave permission to use their photographs. Their names are acknowledged below the donated images. Thank you all.

INTRODUCTION

B efore the word *physics* existed, people perceived natural forces at work in their environment. Knowing that they could not prevent or avoid such phenomena, they tried to understand how the world operated. More than 5,000 years ago, long before any academic institution offered a course in mechanics, men overcame the resistance encountered while dragging a heavy sled by employing the wheel to transport objects. Without knowledge of any mathematical formula to calculate optimal release angles or velocities, a prehistoric man threw a stick with a chiseled stone at its end high in the air to hunt prey from a distance. Just as chemistry describes the composition of the natural world, physics explains how all matter behaves. Defined as the scientific study of matter and energy, physics seeks understanding of natural laws that explain the properties and dictate the actions of everything in the universe from the moons of Jupiter to the scurrying of a mouse behind a stove.

Scientists often partition the subject material of physics into *classical* and *modern* divisions generally based on phenomena explored before and after the turn of the 20th century. Classical physics describes observable phenomena and includes the study of motion, heat and other forms of energy, sound, light, states of matter, electricity, and magnetism. Curiosities of everyday life make sense in light of this knowledge. For example, mechanics describes the advantage provided to a sprinter by setting feet on starting blocks at the beginning of a race. Learning about the properties of the states of matter explains why ice floats. Application of the principles of magnetism and electricity has resulted in inventions, such as air-conditioning and vacuum cleaners, that have transformed society. Modern physics deals mostly with phenomena that occur below the atomic level, such as nuclear decay processes, and with the fundamental particles of matter and their interactions. Pyrotechnicians engineer colorful firework displays based on controlled heating of certain chemical elements that absorb energy in packets and subsequently release photons, a process described by the modern branch of quantum physics. Submarines remain submerged for weeks at a time by using oxygen-independent, nuclear-powered generators, an application of knowledge about how elementary particles interact with each other.

Two different approaches for studying the physical sciences complement each other to advance knowledge in the field. Experimental physicists perform controlled experiments from which they draw conclusions, whereas theoretical physicists use mathematics to describe and to predict events and behavior. Both methods have advantages as well as disadvantages and must be used in conjunction with each other. Theoretical physics allows for exploration of areas beyond the capabilities of available instrumentation or technology upon which experimental physics relies. Confirmation of theoretical predictions comes from experimental results that also guide the theorists as to appropriate pathways for future analysis.

Physics is fundamental to other sciences; its concepts explain phenomena in many disciplines such as biology, chemistry, *astronomy*, and geophysics. Natural laws do not discriminate between living organisms and nonliving things. Biophysics applies the tools of physics to study processes that occur in living organisms. A biophysicist might study the molecular structure of a pigment in order to determine which wavelengths of electromagnetic radiation it absorbs most efficiently. A physical chemist, a scientist who deals with the physical nature of chemical compounds, might calculate the amount of energy required to bind two *atoms* together. Astrophysics considers the physical nature of celestial bodies. An astrophysicist might use spectroscopy to analyze the waves emitted by a star to determine its composition. The combination of physics with geology reveals information such as how processes occurring inside the Earth result in volcanic eruptions or earthquakes that alter the surface of the planet.

During the Renaissance (1300–1600), astronomers paved the way for scientific advances by expanding cultural ideals that favored knowledge. During the Scientific Revolution, an intellectual movement that occurred from 1543 to 1700, philosophers adopted defined objective methods for scientific learning. The advanced technology of the Industrial Revolution, from the late 1700s to the early 1800s, spawned many new scientific instruments and apparatuses. All of these events led to an explosion of advancements in the field of physics over the two centuries that followed.

In 1687, Sir Isaac Newton proposed the law of universal gravitation and established the three laws of motion. He also launched the study of optics by demonstrating that white light is a combination of all colors. A fellow Englishman, Michael Faraday, discovered the phenomenon of electromagnetic induction in 1831, leading to the invention of the electric motor, the generator, and the transformer—three devices that form the foundation of the modern electrical industry. By the end of the 19th century, physicists thought they had learned all the essential principles of physics. The German physicist Max Planck's introduction of the concept of quanta, the notion that energy comes in packages of specific quantities, showed them how wrong they were and led to the development of quantum theory, revolutionizing physics. In 1903, Ernest Rutherford, a physicist from New Zealand, announced a disintegration theory of radioactivity with the remarkable claim that chemical elements transmutate. Through examining this process of radioactive decay, he developed a planetary model for atomic structure that placed orbiting *electrons* outside of a central nucleus.

Pioneering nuclear physicists probed the atomic nucleus to learn more about its structure and contents. After escaping Nazi persecution in Berlin during the late 1930s, Lise Meitner discovered the process of nuclear fission, whereby bombardment of an atomic nucleus causes it to split into two parts. Though the United States asked for her assistance in their efforts to exploit this tendency by developing atomic weapons, she refused. German-born American physicist Albert Einstein also promoted peace later in his life but only after lending his scientific reputation to a plea aimed at convincing the U.S. government that they needed to build atomic weapons to win the Second World War. Einstein had earned his fame decades before when he published several landmark papers in

1905. One explained the nature of light, which he showed existed in packets of energy later called photons, earning him a Nobel Prize. Another proved the existence of molecules by explaining Brownian motion of suspended particles in a liquid. The same year he also published his theory of special relativity, relating the concepts of mass and energy in the famous equation $E = mc^2$ and stating that absolute space and absolute time do not exist. These notions required that the principles of physics be restructured. A little more than a decade later he published his theory of general relativity, which demonstrated the equivalence of gravity and inertia.

Danish physicist Niels Bohr helped usher in the age of quantum physics by updating Rutherford's planetary model for atomic structure with a quantum mechanical model that explained a paradox that classical mechanics could not. Classical physics was proving to be insufficient for explaining many observations at the atomic level and below. Louis de Broglie founded the field of wave mechanics by establishing the dual nature of matter—not only did light exhibit both wave and particle characteristics, but so did matter. Though this bizarre notion seemed to defy common sense, it has endured, and physicists have accepted the limitations of classical physics. When existing theories that attempted to explain the interactions between light and matter continued to fail in the late 1940s, American theoretical physicist Richard Feynman reformulated quantum electrodynamics, sometimes described as the most perfect theory of physics. A few years later his colleague, Murray Gell-Mann, brought organization to the domain of particle physics. The rapid discovery of hundreds of new kinds of subatomic particles had led to mayhem that Gell-Mann settled by proposing the eightfold way, a scheme based on an abstract mathematical model and symmetry properties.

For thousands of years natural philosophers have observed the world around them, hoping to catch a glimpse of nature's secrets. Sometimes nature hesitantly reveals information, and other times a deluge of information spills forth at once, but the pioneering physicists profiled in this book have paid diligent attention. From all that nature has and continues to expose, physicists sort through the data and combine relevant notes, in hopes of one day elucidating all the laws that govern the natural world.

Sir Isaac Newton

(1642–1727)

Sir Isaac Newton's explanations of several natural laws launched the scientific revolution. *(Library of Congress, Prints and Photographs Division [LC-USZ62-101363])*

The Law of Universal Gravitation and Three Laws of Motion

Everyone obeys the natural laws of the universe. Unlike man-made laws, natural laws cannot be broken. They allow for the prediction of the effects of *forces* such as gravity and processes such as motion. While men have been able to predict such consequences and even use natural laws to their advantage for thousands of years, Sir Isaac Newton was the first to use mathematics to prove such laws. He was able to make a connection between the fall of an apple and the organization of the universe. Principles that he delineated in his two major works, *Principia* and *Opticks*, are still used today by all types of scientists and engineers as well as athletes and artists. Newton also invented a branch of mathematics, *calculus*, and made significant contributions to many other areas of mathematics. In addition, he designed the first reflecting telescope, which has allowed the human race to explore further into space than ever before. He has been called the greatest scientist of all time. Who could have guessed that a child expected to die within hours of his birth would revolutionize science and change the world?

No Telltale Signs of Genius

Sir Isaac Newton came into this world prematurely on December 25, 1642, at Woolsthorpe Manor, in Lincolnshire, England. His father, Isaac, was a farmer and had died three months earlier. Three years later his mother, Hannah, was remarried to the much older Reverend Barnabas Smith, who forced her to move to a nearby village, leaving young Isaac with his grandmother. He seems to have had a lonely childhood, perhaps by his own choosing, as he has been described as a serious and somber lad. He began his education at the local school, where he learned to read and write. His free time was spent making models of sundials, windmills, kites, and other such mechanical devices. When he was 10 years old, his stepfather died, and Hannah returned to Woolsthorpe Manor to live with Isaac's three younger half-siblings, Mary, Benjamin, and Hannah.

At age 12, Isaac moved seven miles (11.3 km) away to Grantham and boarded with the Clark family so he could attend the King's Grammar School. Mr. Clark was an *apothecary* (pharmacist), and Isaac learned the basics of chemistry while working in his shop. He performed satisfactorily at school but gave no sign of his hidden genius early on. His study habits are rumored to have improved following a fight with the school's bully, named Arthur Storer, who made very high marks. Isaac was very competitive, and though he won the physical fight, he was determined to beat Arthur in the intellectual realm as well. (Interestingly, Isaac and Arthur corresponded later in life about astronomy.) His schoolmaster began to recognize that Isaac had abilities that could take him beyond his father's farm.

At age 16, Isaac's mother pulled him out of school to run the farm left by his father, but Isaac had no aptitude for farming. Instead of going to market, he would hide out and read all day. Instead of watching the animals, he would sit under a tree and stare into space. The family servants thought he was lazy and dumb. But Isaac's uncle and schoolmaster saw potential in the young man and persuaded Hannah to send him back to school to prepare for college. Perhaps they convinced her he was really a bright boy, or perhaps she was anxious to get him off the farm! At any rate, he reentered school and one year later was admitted to Trinity College at Cambridge University.

Cambridge University

During his first few years of college, Isaac was a sizar, a servant to older students and to faculty in return for reduced fees. The position, in addition to the extra time Isaac had to spend working to earn his stay at Trinity, set him apart from the other students. He had no more close friends in college than he did as a schoolboy. Nevertheless, he was eventually able to find a roommate with whom he shared a similar lifestyle and spent the next four years buried in his books.

One year Isaac went to a nearby fair, where he proceeded to purchase a triangular glass *prism* that was meant to be a child's play toy. He also purchased some books for pleasure reading, including a text on astronomy. To help him understand this, he also purchased a text on Euclidean geometry. After beginning to read it, however, he thought it was silly and bought a more modern text of Descartes's geometry (René Descartes was a famous 17th-century French philosopher). This was much more challenging to comprehend, yet he trudged through it on his own and in the process neglected his regular studies, failing to impress his teachers. He reportedly even failed an exam on Euclidean geometry. During this time, he developed the *binomial theorem*, a shortcut for solving problems where you multiply a binomial (an equation with two variables) by itself many times over, $(a + b)^n$. Of this, the faculty took notice. He began to develop a relationship with Dr. Isaac Barrow, a professor of mathematics. Isaac Newton received his bachelor's degree at age 22, in 1665.

The Miracle Year

Shortly afterward, the bubonic plague took over London. This horrific infectious disease killed about 17,440 people out of London's total population of 93,000. The university was forced to close, and Newton retreated to Woolsthorpe Manor. He may not have wished for a vacation, but by his own recollection the next 18 months turned out to be the most intellectually productive of his life. This time period is often referred to by scholars as *annus mirabilis*, or the "miracle year."

During this time, Newton continued playing with prisms. He explored the relationship between *light* and color. Prisms are intriguing toys because when light hits them, they create a rainbow of colors. Scientists thought this might be because the light that entered them was dirtied or darkened as it passed through the glass itself. Newton wondered about this and the nature of light, which was a hot topic at the time. To explore light, he darkened his room, letting only a small beam of light through the window. This light was aimed at the prism, which had a black screen behind it. The light splayed onto the screen in the expected rainbow of colors. Newton wondered why the shape of the light emitted onto the screen was oblong in shape, whereas the light hitting it was just a small circle in shape. He then set a second prism upside down between the first prism and the screen, not knowing what to expect. Surprisingly, the rainbow disappeared, and white light was restored. He also isolated single colors of light from the *spectrum* by using a board with a tiny hole in it and sent those colored beams of light through a second prism onto the screen. When individual col-

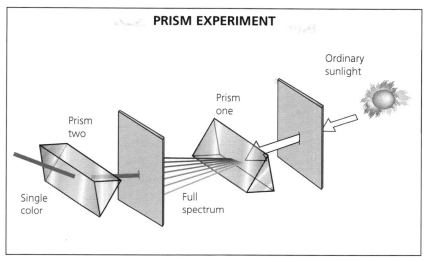

PRISM EXPERIMENT

Ordinary
sunlight

Prism
one

Prism
two

Single
color

Full
spectrum

Newton demonstrated that white light contained all the colors of the spectrum.

ors were sent through the second prism, the same single color shone on the screen. He concluded that each individual color was a component of white light—white light was due to the presence of all the colors. This was contrary to the popular belief that white light was due to the absence of any color. What was happening was that the individual colors were refracted or bent by the prism to different degrees; the red was bent the least, and the blue light was bent the most. Thus a circle of white light entered the prism and exited as an elongated spectrum of the individual colors.

Newton was also intrigued by the principles and mathematics of motion. There was no method for solving certain equations concerning motion because variables changed as rates of speed changed. Thus he developed the foundation of a new type of mathematics he called "fluxions." Today we call this branch of mathematics calculus, and it is concerned with solving problems that have ever-changing variables. He used these new methods in many of his mathematical proofs.

The German astronomer Johannes Kepler had proposed that planets orbited elliptically around the Sun, that their speed changed during their *orbits*, and that the length of time it took to

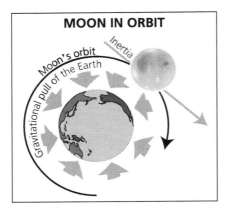

MOON IN ORBIT

Moon's orbit

Inertia

Gravitational pull of the Earth

The Earth's gravitational pull keeps the Moon orbiting the planet rather than traveling off into space, as inertia alone predicts.

complete one orbit was related to the distance the planet was located from the Sun. Newton was learned in Kepler's Laws concerning planetary motion, but he wondered what kept the planets, and the Moon for that matter, in orbit? He spent a lot of time pondering this question, and one day as he sat under an apple tree, his mind was primed to discover the law of universal *gravitation*. A piece of fruit fell to the ground, and Newton contemplated why it fell downward. Was the Earth pulling the apple toward itself? He proposed the existence of an attractive force that acted between all pieces of *matter*. This force of gravity depended on the *masses* of the bodies involved (for example, the apple and the Earth) and the distances between them. Perhaps, he mused, the same force attracts the Moon, but then why does it not fall to Earth like the apple does? The Moon is kept balanced by its attraction to the Earth and *inertia*. Thus it is being pulled downward and sideways at the same time, keeping it in orbit.

Newton started working out mathematical calculations of the Earth's pull on the Moon as well as the *elliptical* orbits of the planets, but his estimation for the radius of the Earth was incorrect. In addition, he was not sure whether to use the Earth's surface or center as the center of gravity's pull. Thus he was unable to completely finish this proof. Frustrated, he set it aside, but he never forgot about it. As time would have it, 18 months after his productive holiday began, Cambridge University reopened following the Great Fire of London, which ended the plague by killing all the rats that were spreading it.

Newton returned to London and, at age 25, began working on a master's degree, which he completed in 1668. The lifestyle of a research fellow suited him. He had plenty of time to study inde-

Newton's reflecting telescope used mirrors to concentrate and reflect light. *(Science Source/ Photo Researchers, Inc.)*

pendently and could live at the university. Two years later, Professor Barrow resigned, and Newton replaced him as a professor of mathematics at Trinity College.

Newton continued his studies of *optics*. One problem with the common reflecting telescopes of the time was chromatic aberration. This means that the observed images were surrounded by rings of color that blurred the image. He devised a telescope that replaced a second convex lens with an angled mirror to focus the light on the eyepiece to reduce the effects of chromatic aberration. In addition, he put the eyepiece on the side of the telescope rather than the end, making it more comfortable to use. He showed this reflecting telescope to Professor Barrow, who took it to London in 1671 to show it off. He brought one to the premier academic

Robert Hooke

Robert Hooke (July 18, 1635–March 3, 1703) was an eminent 17th-century English scientist who contributed to a broad range of developing fields, including physics, astronomy, and microbiology. Few of his accomplishments can be discussed without also mentioning other scientists, and most often, these associations were not friendly.

Hooke attended Oxford University, where he worked in the laboratory of British physicist and chemist Robert Boyle. Being mechanically inclined, Hooke made improvements to the air pump that Boyle used while performing the famous research leading to Boyle's gas law, which states that the pressure and volume of gas are inversely proportional at a constant temperature.

Hooke was an eminent microscopist and, in 1665, he published *Micrographia,* a book that contained hundreds of intricate sketches of specimens, such as insects, bird feathers, and fossils, that he viewed under a microscope. The Dutch microbiologist Antoni van Leeuwenhoek, who discovered microscopic life, might have been inspired by drawings from this book. When the Royal Society of London received correspondence from Leeuwenhoek describing his unbelievable discovery of animalcules, Hooke was the one who repeated the experiments and verified their existence. A famous observation made by Hooke was the presence of rec-

organization, the Royal Society of London, whose members were so impressed that the next year they elected Newton a member. Modern astronomers still use reflecting telescopes to gather astronomical data.

Excited to finally have an audience for his scientific musings, Newton presented his experiments on light that led to his inven-

tangular-shaped holes in thinly sliced cork that reminded him of cells in a monastery. Since Hooke's discovery, the cell has become accepted as the basic unit of life.

When Newton published a paper in 1672 proposing that light traveled in *waves*, similar to waves on water, Hooke complained that Newton stole his idea. The two men fought bitterly over this for decades. Their disdain for one another was fueled further when Newton published his theory of universal gravitation in 1686, and Hooke claimed priority credit for the inverse square law, the fact that the attraction between the Sun and the Earth varied inversely as the square of the distance from the Sun. The truth is Hooke's theory was incomplete, and Hooke was unable to prove it mathematically whereas Newton did.

Interested in flight and the elasticity of air, Hooke also researched the property of elasticity, the ability of a body to be restored to its original shape after distortion. He proposed what has become known as Hooke's law, which states that the power or restoring force of a spring or elastic body is proportional to the length it is extended. More generally, stress is directly proportional to strain; the more a rubber band is stretched, the greater the force unleashed when it snaps back to its original length. Hooke also used his knowledge of springs to create spring-based chronometers for keeping time much more accurately than previous pendulum-based systems. He was unsuccessful in finding investors for his invention, however, and the Dutch physicist and astronomer Christiaan Huygens patented his own version more than a decade later. Priority credit for this invention remains unresolved.

tion of the reflecting telescope to the Royal Society. At the time, the English physicist Robert Hooke was the curator of experiments for the society. Hooke had previously performed similar experiments with light, though less extensive and not as explanatory as Newton's. Hooke took offense that some of the comments Newton made in his paper disagreed with some of Hooke's own beliefs, and a lifelong bitterness between Newton and Hooke ensued. Newton was furious at having to defend the validity of his conclusions and vowed never again to publish his findings.

A Hidden Proof

Newton continued living his solitary and studious lifestyle. As a professor at Cambridge, he was required to give weekly lectures. He was not a popular speaker, however, and his lectures were not well attended. Much of his time was spent privately studying *alchemy*. Alchemy was a shady business concerned with the alteration of ordinary metals into gold and the preparation of a magic elixir that would extend life. While it was an early form of chemistry, it was regarded mostly as wizardry at the time. Newton's interest in alchemy was probably based on his interest in the nature of matter and of life. He most likely would have been embarrassed if his contemporaries found out about his secret studies. This was not a problem, though, since he did not collaborate much and was a loner.

As a member of the Royal Society, Newton corresponded regularly with Hooke, who now was secretary and in charge of keeping abreast of the members' activities. Through this correspondence, Newton was reminded of his earlier calculations concerning elliptical orbits of the planets. He now had access to the correct value for the Earth's radius and was able to complete the solution to this problem successfully. Because Newton recognized the significance of this accomplishment, he was extremely excited. Rumor has it he had to have an assistant finish writing down the calculations because he was too anxious himself. However, he was still hesitant to share his work with others since he had been publicly harassed by Hooke years before. Thus he proceeded to shove his amazing proof in a drawer.

Years later, in 1684, while Newton remained hidden away in his lab, three other members of the Royal Society, Hooke, Christopher Wren, and Edmond Halley, were discussing the problem of elliptical orbits while drinking coffee together. They had figured out that the force needed to move planets in a circle around the Sun obeyed the inverse square law. This meant that a planet twice as far from the Sun would only require one-fourth the force exerted by the Sun to keep it in orbit. But these three extremely intelligent men could not figure out why they traveled in elliptical orbits. After months without success, Halley set out to visit Newton. He was shocked when he presented the problem to Newton only to hear Newton remark that he had solved that problem 15 years ago. This was an amazing accomplishment, and Halley could hardly believe Newton had kept it to himself. However, Newton could not locate the calculations immediately. He promised to redo them and send them as soon as possible. Several months later, Newton mailed his proof to Halley. By 1686, Newton had fleshed out the nine-page proof into his most famous work, which described the workings of the universe using mathematics.

Magnificent *Principia*

The full title of this work is *The Mathematical Principles of Natural Philosophy*, though it is most often referred to by the abbreviation of its Latin name, *Principia*. It was a three-volume work that almost was not published, as the Royal Society was short on funds. Halley himself arranged the financial support for the publication of this work. In addition, Hooke again was angered, claiming that Newton stole his ideas. Newton balked, but Halley smoothed things over, and the world is forever in his debt.

The first volume of *Principia* described what are known today as the three laws of motion. The first law summarizes inertia, the tendency originally articulated by the Italian astronomer and mathematician Galileo Galilei: an object in motion remains in motion at a constant speed in a straight line, and an object at rest remains at rest unless acted upon by an outside force. Because air resistance and *friction* act upon most earthly motions, if you kick a ball, it eventually will stop. The second law of motion states that force is equal to the product of mass and *acceleration*. This law explains why it is harder to throw a bowling ball than a tennis ball. The third law maintains that for every action, there is an equal and opposite reaction. When one object exerts a force on another object, the second object exerts an equal but opposite force on the first. For example, when someone pushes off the ground to jump vertically, the force their feet place on the ground is equal to the force that the ground is exerting back onto their feet.

Using these laws, Newton calculated the gravitational force between the Earth and the Moon, proving that it followed the inverse square law; the force was directly proportional to the product of the two masses (the mass of the Earth × the mass of the Moon) and inversely proportional to the square of the distance between the centers of the Earth and the Moon. Previously, it had been assumed that the universe and the Earth followed different sets of natural laws. Amazingly, Newton went on to prove that his predictions concerning gravitational forces could be applied throughout the universe. Thus Newton was able to explain mathematically Kepler's laws of planetary motion and demonstrate why the planets orbited the Sun in elliptical rather than circular pathways.

In the second volume of *Principia*, Newton disproved Descartes's explanation of planetary motion. He had proposed that the universe was filled with a fluid that was whirlpooling the planets and the stars around the universe by its vortex motion. While many people accepted this explanation, Newton disproved it mathematically.

Before the third and last volume of *Principia* was published, Newton became annoyed and sulky due to Hooke's claims that he deserved credit for discovering the inverse square law. Newton almost refused to continue. Halley panicked, worried that the first two volumes would not sell as well without the third volume completed and that society would never receive this wonderful contribution Newton was capable of making. Luckily, he was again able to smooth things over. The third volume applied Newton's new theories to the Moon, planets, and comets. It contained predictions using the laws of motion and gravity, which he formulated. One prediction he made was that gravity should cause Earth to be a perfect sphere, but the rotation of the Earth about its axis should cause a bulge at the equator. Newton predicted the size of this bulge; it has since proven correct to within 1 percent accuracy. He also predicted that comets would follow elliptical paths just like planets but that they would have more elongated paths. Halley was quite excited by the realization that the motion of comets could be predicted using Newton's laws. Credited for discovering Halley's Comet, he was able to use Newton's laws and methods to predict the return of this comet every 76 years. It has returned every 76 years hence.

Life Outside of Academics

Later in his life, Newton became more involved in both university and national politics. In 1689, he was elected to Parliament. This was shortly after the "Glorious Revolution," when King James II fled to France and Prince William of Holland took over. During this year, Newton voted to make William and Mary the king and queen of England, in favor of the Bill of Rights that gave more power to the citizens of England, and for the Toleration Act that allowed more religious freedom.

In 1693, Isaac Newton suffered a mental breakdown. He started writing weird letters to his friends and accused them of plotting against him and making odd threats. These episodes might have resulted from overwork, as people who knew him recalled that he often forgot to eat or sleep when he was in the midst of a scientific breakthrough. Or perhaps his antagonistic personality and the stress from the continual controversy surrounding the intellectual ownership of his work wore him down. A more recent explanation suggests that he was suffering mercury poisoning from his experiments in alchemy.

By 1696, he seemed completely recovered. He was offered an administrative position as warden of the Royal Mint, which was in charge of producing the currency. When he took this position, it was supposed to be a reward, mostly in title, but Newton was a hard worker. The nation was having a coin crisis. The coins in circulation were being clipped and the precious metal melted down for other uses. Moreover, the design was easy to duplicate, making counterfeiting too easy. Under Newton's commission, all the old coins were recalled and replaced with a newer coin with a more intricate design and a less precious composition. In 1700, he was named master of the Mint and, in 1701, he resigned his position as professor at Cambridge.

Around this time he moved out of the warden's house at the Mint and into his own home with his niece, Catherine Barton, who served as his hostess. Newton only attended Royal Society meetings occasionally, as he hated facing Hooke. After Hooke's death in 1703, Newton was elected president of the Royal Society, a position to which he was reelected every year until his death 23 years later. During his tenure he brought the society financial security and offered encouragement for many new scientists.

With the Mint running smoothly and his archenemy gone forever, he began composing another masterpiece, *Opticks*. This book described his earlier experiments on light and color and formed the basis of the field of *spectroscopy*, the study of light. He also began writing updated revisions of *Principia*. To accomplish this, he corresponded with John Flamsteed to obtain current astronomical data. Newton was not generous in his explanation for needing this data, thus Flamsteed was wary of sharing all this information. In addition, some of Flamsteed's figures were incorrect figures, which irritated Newton, who had to repeat his calculations.

Hooke and Flamsteed were not Newton's only foes. The German mathematician Gottfried Wilhelm Leibniz argued with Newton over who invented calculus first. Actually, Leibniz published his results before Newton, but Newton may have arrived at them first while formulating his theory of universal gravitation. Newton's powerful position as president of the Royal Society and his international reputation were no match for Leibniz, so Newton received credit for this achievement.

Death of Sir Isaac

Queen Anne knighted Newton in 1705. He was the first scientist to receive such an honor. In January 1725, his health began to deteriorate. He moved out to Kensington (which used to be outside of

London) in hopes of healing a cough. He died on March 20, 1727, at age 84 and was buried at Westminster Abbey.

Remarkable as he was, Newton was not always right about everything. For example, he thought that light was composed of bunches of corpuscles that were ejected from the light source. By the 1800s most scientists believed in the wave theory of light, as did Robert Hooke. However, in the 20th century, when the theoretical physicist Albert Einstein described *photons* as being particles of light, many similarities were noted between them and Newton's corpuscles. Newton also did experiments in 1717 that he believed demonstrated the existence of ether. Ether was a mysterious invisible substance believed to fill all space. Its existence was disproved in 1887 by Albert Michelson and Edward Morley.

The verse inscribed at the bottom of a monument erected in his honor reads, "Let mortals rejoice that there has existed so great an Ornament to the Human Race." Very few scientists have been so successful at unlocking nature's secrets. Not only was Newton an amazing puzzle solver, but he was also methodical, meticulous in his calculations and record keeping, and he recognized the significance of his numerous discoveries. While not many people are capable of understanding his original works, everyone should appreciate the huge impact he has had on the maturation of science. His research shaped the pinnacle of the Scientific Revolution. Before Newton, scientists relied heavily on conjecture and assumptions made by Greek philosophers hundreds and thousands of years prior. After Newton, scientists starting doubting claims; they began to believe only that which they observed. They began to test hypotheses, many times over, before drawing conclusions. Newton was able to explain in mathematical language, very logically and concretely, that which had amazed and awed generations for thousands of years—the workings of the universe. He may not have had many friends among his contemporaries, but he was respected by all, feared by some, and inspirational to the upcoming scientists.

CHRONOLOGY

1642	Sir Isaac Newton is born December 25th at Woolsthorpe Manor, Lincolnshire
1661	Enrolls at Trinity College, Cambridge University
1665	Returns to Woolsthorpe during plague outbreak in London
1665–66	Time period known as *annus mirabilis*, or "miracle year"
1667	Becomes a fellow at Trinity College
1686	Earns a master's degree from Cambridge University
1669	Becomes professor of mathematics at Trinity College
1672	Publishes *A New Theory of Light and Colors*
1684	Returns to the study of gravity
1687	Publishes *The Mathematical Principles of Natural Philosophy* (also known as its Latin abbreviation, *Principia*), which described the three laws of motion and the law of universal gravitation and explained planetary motion
1689	Becomes a member of Parliament
1693	Suffers nervous breakdown
1696	Becomes warden of the Royal Mint in London
1700	Becomes master of the Mint
1701	Resigns as professor at Cambridge University
1703–27	Serves as president of the Royal Society
1704	Publishes *Opticks*, describing his experiments on light and color
1705	Newton is knighted by Queen Anne, becoming the first scientist to receive such an honor
1727	Dies March 20th at age 84, in Kensington, and is buried at Westminster Abbey

FURTHER READING

Allaby, Michael, and Derek Gjertsen. *Makers of Science.* Vol. 1. New York: Oxford University Press, 2002. Chronological biographies of influential scientists. Includes political and social settings as well as scientific achievements.

British Broadcasting Corporation. "Historic Figures: Sir Isaac Newton (1643–1727)," Available online. URL: http://www.bbc.co.uk/history/historic_figures/newton_isaac.shtml. Accessed on January 28, 2005. Part of a series from the BBC. Contains biographical information and discusses scientific accomplishments.

Fauvel, John, Raymond Flood, Michael Shorthand, and Robin Wilson, eds. *Let Newton Be!* New York: Oxford University Press, 1988. Collection of essays written from different perspectives about Newton's quirks and ingenuities.

Giants of Science: Isaac Newton, Charles Darwin, Louis Pasteur. New York: Marshall Cavendish Corporation, 1991. Contains several illustrations of Newton and his work. For juvenile readers.

Gillispie, Charles C., ed. *Dictionary of Scientific Biography.* Vol. 10. New York: Scribner, 1970–76. Good source for facts concerning personal background and scientific accomplishments but assumes reader has basic knowledge of science.

Spangenburg, Ray, and Diane K. Moser. *The Birth of Science: Ancient Times to 1699.* New York: Facts On File, 2004. Outlines the history of science, building on the ideas of great minds and their predecessors. Intended for middle and high school students.

2

Michael Faraday

(1791–1867)

The electrical industry was built upon principles discovered by Michael Faraday. *(Science Source/Photo Researchers, Inc.)*

Discovery of Electromagnetic Induction

Most people do not lay awake at night wondering what scientific principle allows electrical *energy* to be transformed into the rotational motion of the fan in their blow dryer. How does that *electricity* get into the home anyhow? Until one goes camping in the woods, he or she probably does not think much about the conveniences permitted by the modern electrical industry. One man is responsible for the three inventions upon which the electrical industry is built: the electric motor, the *generator*, and the *transformer*. His name was Michael Faraday, and his contributions extend beyond that of simplifying lives through modern conveniences such as vacuum cleaners and ceiling fans. He made important contributions to the fields of chemistry and physics as well. He was a simple man born to an unknown family, but his creative intelligence and desire to learn led him out of the slums of London into the most respected intellectual societies in Europe. His research led the Industrial Revolution out of the factories of Great Britain and into the households of common man.

Humble Beginnings

The Faradays had just moved to Newington Butts (now part of London) when their third child, Michael, was born on September 22, 1791. James Faraday was a skilled blacksmith but suffered from rheumatism and was often too ill to work. So when Margaret gave birth to their fourth child in 1802, the family was living in poverty. Later in life Michael recalled having only a single loaf of bread to live on for an entire week. When he was 13 years old, he found a job as an errand boy for a local bookbinder named George Riebau. In those days and especially in his neighborhood, many people could not afford to subscribe to the newspaper, so several people often shared one. One of Michael's jobs was to deliver the paper, then fetch it and deliver it to the next customer.

Mr. Riebau appreciated Michael's work ethic and offered him an apprenticeship when he was 14 years old. Over the next seven years Michael learned to pack pages, sew them together, and cover them with leather. He lived at Riebau's store with several other apprentices, but Michael was different. For one thing, he carried around a self-improvement text in his pocket. In addition, he devoured every book that he bound. He took notes from many of them and bound them in a special notebook, and he asked lots of questions. Hearing the answers was not enough for young Michael. He needed to test them and prove for himself that the explanation worked.

Michael was particularly curious about electricity. He had read a treatise on electricity in the *Encyclopaedia Britannica* that had passed through Riebau's shop. He was also engrossed by Jane Marcet's *Conversations on Chemistry* text. With permission from his employer, he set up a little lab in his bedroom to duplicate experiments he read about. To quench his thirst for scientific knowledge, in 1810 he started attending meetings of the City Philosophical Society. This organization was a sort of intellectual club, where ordinary men could assemble to discuss scientific matters. Sometimes they sponsored lectures by famous scientists. Riebau's customers knew Michael. One was so impressed by Michael's desire to learn that, in 1812, he offered him tickets to the final four lectures in a series given by a famous English chemist, Sir Humphry Davy.

Assistant to Davy

Davy was a professor of chemistry at the Royal Institution (RI) of Great Britain, an organization that supports scientific research and teaching. He was well-known for discovering that electricity could be used to liberate metals from *compounds* and for discovering the gas nitrous oxide. He was a popular, entertaining lecturer. Faraday was engrossed by his discourses and recopied all of his lecture notes neatly onto fresh paper, illustrated them, and bound them. The end of his apprenticeship was drawing near, and he worried about his future. He had a job lined up with a bookbinder in town, but by now Faraday knew he wanted to be a scientist.

Bookbinding was boring to Faraday. Business seemed corrupt. He was a deeply religious young man, raised in a Sandemanian church. Sandemanians were a sect of Protestants that took the Bible literally and did not believe in the accumulation of material possessions. They honored simplicity, peace, and humility. Faraday believed that scientists were pure, that they were somehow morally superior to other people, especially businessmen, and he wanted to join their faction. By a strange twist of fate, Davy was temporarily blinded in a lab explosion in 1812. Someone recommended that he ask Faraday to serve as his secretary for a few days. Shortly thereafter, Faraday sent Davy the nearly 400-page bound volume of

Davy's Intoxicating Discovery

Some have suggested that Sir Humphry Davy's greatest discovery was Michael Faraday, but he made many significant contributions to science in the early 19th century. He pioneered the field of *electrochemistry* and used electricity to break down many compounds to their elemental components. He discovered many *elements,* including sodium, potassium, magnesium, calcium, strontium, and barium. He also showed that the gas formed from muriatic acid (today called hydrogen chloride, HCl) was composed of hydrogen and an unidentified substance that he named chlorine.

As director of the laboratory of the Pneumatic Institute at Clifton, he often experimented on himself to ascertain whether a particular gas had therapeutic effects. Once he almost suffocated after inhaling four quarts of hydrogen gas. Another gas, however, had a more pleasant effect. Nitrous oxide (N_2O) was discovered by English chemist Joseph Priestley in the late 18th century. When inhaled, the gas made Davy feel euphoric and uninhibited. He also noticed that pain he suffered from an erupted wisdom tooth abated under the intoxicating effect of the gas. In 1799, Davy published a book characterizing nitrous oxide and describing its effects. Inhalation of nitrous oxide, which is also called laughing gas, soon became a popular recreational activity. Davy's suggestion of using nitrous oxide as an anesthetic went ignored for over four decades. As a mild analgesic and sedative, today it is used in dentistry to reduce pain and relieve patient anxiety.

his lecture notes with a request for a position. Davy was impressed, but no position was available. Faraday was disappointed.

Several months later, a laboratory assistant at the RI was fired for fighting. Davy recommended Faraday for the spot, and in March 1813, at the age of 21 years, Michael Faraday started working for the RI as a chemical assistant. His duties included assisting Davy in his laboratory research, maintaining the equipment, and helping professors in their lecture preparation. The pay was lower than he made as a bookbinder, but Faraday felt he was in heaven. He remained associated with the RI until his retirement.

After only six months, Faraday left London to tour Europe with Davy and his wife. During the extended trip, Davy discovered the new element iodine. Faraday witnessed Davy's genius firsthand and had the opportunity to meet with many other scientists. Though his role was officially that of scientific assistant and secretary, Faraday was treated more like a servant, especially by Lady Davy. He was anxious for the trip to be over.

Upon his return to London in 1815, he worked very long hours. He certainly did not make time to socialize. In 1816, he started lecturing at the City Philosophical Society. He formulated his own concept of a philosopher, which he preferred to the newer, more specialized terms of *physicist* or *chemist*. He felt strongly that philosophers should remain open-minded and objective. He criticized philosophers who performed experiments in order to prove something they already believed to be true. Instead, he felt philosophers should conduct experiments to test hypotheses objectively.

One of Faraday's first true scientific explorations was to help Davy study the dangerous problem of coal miner safety from gas explosions. The problem stemmed from the workers illuminating the mines by using naked flames. They found that by enclosing the flame in wire gauze, the *heat* from the flame would be absorbed by the wire and not ignite the methane. Thus the Davy lamp was invented. Shortly thereafter, in 1816, Faraday published his first of many scientific papers entitled, "Analysis of Native Caustic Lime of Tuscany" in the *Quarterly Journal of Science*.

Faraday was becoming indispensable at the RI. He worked long hours and published numerous reports. His abilities as a lecturer also greatly improved. He did not have time to socialize but attended church every Sunday, and there he met a friend's sister, Sarah

Barnard. He was mesmerized by her, and she listened attentively to him talk excitedly about his philosophies on life. It turns out he was a talented poet, and he enticed the young Sarah into marrying him in 1821. She moved with Faraday into the RI, where they lived for 46 years. Shortly after their union, Faraday officially made his confession of faith in the Sandemanian Church.

His chemical researches early on involved producing and analyzing new chemical compounds, such as those consisting of carbon and chlorine, and studying metallurgy. He worked to make higher grade steel alloys. This task was laborious, but Faraday kept current in scientific literature. Two decades prior, Italian physicist Alessandro Giuseppe Antonio Anastasio, conte Volta had invented the first electric battery, called a *voltaic pile*, by stacking discs of copper, zinc, and cardboard soaked in salt water, then attaching a wire from the top to bottom. This produced a steady flow of electric current. One important more recent discovery by Danish physicist Hans Christian Ørsted was that electricity had a *magnetic field*. This was exceptional because the needle of a magnetic compass was deflected at right angles to the wire carrying an electric current, suggesting that the magnetic force produced by an electric current acted in a circle rather than a straight line.

Construction of the First Electric Motor

In 1821, another English scientist named William Hyde Wollaston visited Davy's laboratory. He attempted to rotate a wire that was carrying an electric current on its axis by using a magnet. This got Faraday thinking. He devised an apparatus that would convert electric energy into mechanical motion. The device consisted of two bowls of mercury, which is an electric *conductor*. A battery was attached below the bowls to metal rods inserted into the bottom of each bowl. A metal bar dipped into the tops of both bowls to complete the circuit. One bowl had a fixed upright magnet and a movable wire hanging into the mercury, and the other bowl had a fixed upright wire and a movable magnet hanging into the bowl. When the current was turned on, the movable wire circled the stationary magnet in the first bowl, and the movable magnet rotated about the

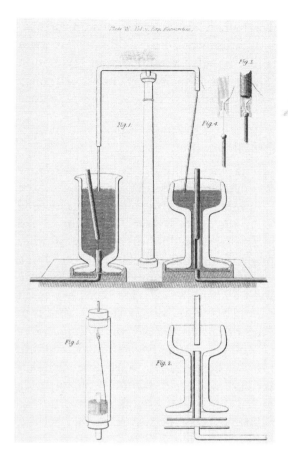

Electrical energy was converted into mechanical motion in the first motor. *(Library of Congress, Prints and Photographs Division [LC-USZ62-95340])*

fixed wire in the second bowl. Faraday had transformed an electric current into a continuous mechanical motion, creating the first electric motor. His publication, "On Some New Electro-Magnetical Motions, and on the Theory of Magnetism," in the *Quarterly Journal of Science* (1821), reported these investigations and contained the first mention of a line of force that encircled the current-carrying wire. This viewpoint was different from that of most scientists at the time who thought of electricity as a fluid through which particles carrying electrical energy flowed.

Unfortunately, this amazing accomplishment was darkened by a mistake that Faraday later regretted. When he reported his results, he failed to give any credit to Davy or Wollaston. Faraday defended himself by saying that Wollaston had been trying to make a current-carrying wire rotate on its own axis when held near a magnet, and anyhow, Wollaston had failed. Faraday was successful. Wollaston was more forgiving than Davy, but Faraday was always extremely careful from then on to give any credit where it was rightfully due.

Growing Reputation

In 1823, Faraday was working with chlorine hydrate, and Davy suggested he heat the *crystals* in a closed tube. When he did so, the crystals melted, and as the pressure built up inside the enclosed tube an oily liquid collected in the opposite arm. He had produced liquid chlorine. He attempted this procedure on a variety of other gases, such as carbon dioxide, with similar results. While doing this, he became the first scientist to create temperatures below 0°F (−17.8°C) in the laboratory. Incidentally, he injured his eye in an explosion during these experiments. Faraday reported his results in two papers submitted to the *Philosophical Transactions of the Royal Society*. Before publishing them, Davy added a statement crediting himself with the suggestion. These results were extraordinary because scientists were not sure some gases could exist in more than one state. Even though Davy was Faraday's mentor, he was jealous of all the attention that his protégé was receiving. In fact, the next year when Faraday was elected as a fellow of the Royal Society, Davy (then the president of the Royal Society) opposed his nomination!

Faraday often did private consulting work and donated his earnings back to the RI's research funds. He was often solicited for advice on chemical matters from the Royal Engineers, the Royal Artillery, and the Admiralty. He also taught chemistry at the Royal Military Academy from 1829 to 1853. During the decades he worked for the RI, he served as a court expert witness, helped lighthouses burn fuel more efficiently, and performed chemical analyses for gas companies. In 1825, he was sent a sample for chemical analysis. After skillfully investigating the substance, he concluded it was a compound made of carbon and hydrogen, which he called bicarburet of hydrogen. This was Faraday's greatest contribution to the field of chemistry. Today we call this compound benzene, and its utility in organic chemistry is immeasurable. It is utilized in the production of nylon, polystyrene, and rubber.

Also in 1825, the Royal Society assigned Faraday to a project aimed at improving the quality of optical glass, such as glass used to make telescope lenses. He worked on this for about five years, during which time he made modest advances. However, he obtained an assistant named Sergeant Charles Anderson who remained Faraday's only assistant for 40 years.

Faraday's successes as an independent researcher brought with them more responsibilities and duties. In 1825, he was appointed director of the laboratory at the RI. He had begun giving private lectures at the RI in 1824, and three years later started lecturing publicly. In 1826, as director, Faraday helped found the Friday Evening Discourses that continue today. Members of the RI and their guests gather to hear prominent scientists explain current theory and research in their fields in layman's terms. Faraday gave 123 of these lectures. Around the same time, Faraday initiated another series of lectures called the Christmas Lectures for children, during which famous scientists explain complex scientific topics and demonstrate experiments for children over the Christmas holiday. Faraday himself gave 19 of these lectures, including his most famous, "The Chemical History of the Candle."

Davy's health deteriorated, and he died in 1827. Despite their differences, Faraday had great respect for Davy and always spoke of him with reverence and fondness. He was deeply saddened by his passing. He felt a great loyalty to Davy and to the RI. When he was offered a professorship in chemistry at the new London University, he declined.

Michael and Sarah Faraday never had any children of their own, but they raised a niece from the age of 10 years. Faraday enjoyed children, as was evident by his commitment to his Christmas lectures and the quality playtime he spent with his niece. He and his wife attended theater performances and went on summer holidays, but Faraday avoided social engagements outside of his own family as much as possible. Unless an invitation was from a president of the Royal Society, he usually declined.

Electromagnetic Research

By 1831, Faraday felt confident enough that after completing his report on optical glass, he could work on subjects of his own choosing. He was anxious to further experiment with *electromagnetism*. Physicists knew that electricity could produce *magnetism*, but he wondered if the reverse was also true—could magnetism be used to create an electric current? After much thought on how to test this, he wrapped one side of an iron ring with an insulated copper wire attached to a voltaic battery. On the other side, he wound another wire attached to a *galvanometer* to detect an electrical current. When the final connection was made, the needle jumped and then rested again. Starting a current in one coil magnetized the iron ring, which then induced an electrical current in the other wire, as detected by the galvanometer. When the current was turned off, the needle momentarily jumped again and then rested. To make sure what he saw was real, he repeated his experiment using a more sensitive measuring device, ensuring there were no leaks of current or metallic connections between the two wires. It appeared that only changes in the magnetic field generated an electric current. Also, the voltage in the second coil depended not only on the power from the battery, but also on the number of coils in the wire. One could alter the voltage by changing the number of turns in the coil.

A few months later, Faraday performed a similar experiment using a magnetic rod that he moved in and out of a solenoid formed from a copper wire. The ends of the wire were connected to a galvanometer. When the magnet or the solenoid was moved, a current was detected. When the relationship between the two objects was stationary, no current was detected. Though he was successful in inducing a current, he expected it to be continuous. Faraday's thoughts returned to lines of force that he imagined surrounded the magnet. These lines are invisible but can be visualized by sprinkling iron shavings onto a piece of paper held over a magnet. The shavings line up in definite patterns surrounding the magnet. Only when the lines of force moved and crossed the wire did they create an electric current in it.

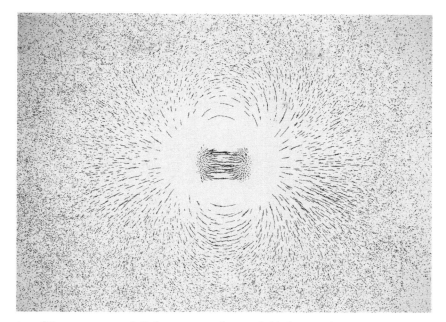

Iron filings assume a definite pattern when sprinkled over a bar magnet, allowing the lines of force of the magnetic field to be visualized. *(Vaughan Fleming/Science Photo Library/Photo Researchers, Inc.)*

He next set up a copper disc so that its edge passed between the poles of a horseshoe-shaped magnet. A wire connected the axle at the center of the disc to the edge of the disc. A galvanometer was attached to detect the presence of a current. When the disc was spun, a continuous current was produced between the center of the disk and its edge. Motion had been converted into electricity.

Faraday presented these results to the Royal Society in November 1831. These experiments allowed Faraday to conclude that a changing magnetic field can produce an electric current, a process called *electromagnetic induction* (or *electrical induction*). Around the same time, the American physicist Joseph Henry also discovered electrical induction, but Faraday published his results first, so he is given credit. (His results appeared in *Philosophical Transactions* in 1832.) One of the most common uses of electromagnetic induction

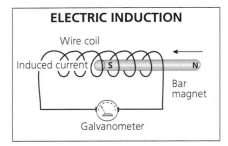

ELECTRIC INDUCTION

Wire coil

Induced current

Bar magnet

Galvanometer

Moving a magnet through a coiled wire produced an electric current.

today is in generators (also called dynamos). A magnetic field inside the generator causes a wire coil to spin rapidly, creating an electric current that is then sent to homes or other buildings that use electricity. Thus generators convert mechanical energy (movement) into electric energy. Transformers also operate on the principle of induction. Transformers are devices used to increase or decrease voltage (the measure of the electric force of

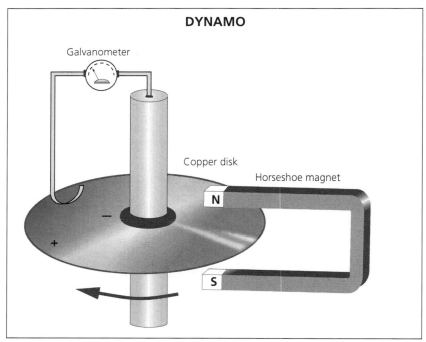

DYNAMO

Galvanometer

Copper disk

Horseshoe magnet

N

S

Rotation of a copper disc produced an electrical current from mechanical motion in the first dynamo.

a current). For example, electric power plants create extremely high-voltage currents, but only low-voltage currents are needed to run ordinary household appliances such as lamps or toasters.

Faraday wondered if the sort of electricity that he created through the use of magnets was the same as static electricity or electricity produced from a voltaic pile. He searched the literature and performed a series of tests that showed the same effects resulted no matter what the electrical source, thus electricity was electricity. While the intensity might vary, the nature was all the same.

Electrochemistry and Light

Over the next few years, Faraday merged his knowledge of chemistry with the developing field of electricity. Years before, Davy had figured out how to separate metals by passing an electric current through them. Faraday called this process *electrolysis*, the chemical decomposition of a compound by sending an electric current through it. In 1833, he established two basic laws of electrolysis. The first law stated that the quantity of metal liberated was proportional to the quantity of electricity used. The second law stated that the electricity required to liberate the unit equivalent mass of any element was precisely the same. To describe his research, he had to make up several new words, including anode, cathode, *electrode*, electrolyte, anion, and cation. These are now an essential part of scientific vocabulary.

In 1833, Michael Faraday was named the first Fullerian Professor of Chemistry at the RI for his advances in electrochemistry. He began to collect many other honors and medals at this time, including two Copley medals from the Royal Society (1832, 1838), an honorary doctorate from Oxford, membership in the Senate of the University of London, and more. In 1836, he was named scientific advisor for Trinity House, which was in charge of maintaining safe waterways in England and Wales and overseeing the lighthouses.

By 1835, his research in electrochemistry led him to consider electrostatics. He had found that electrochemical forces were intermolecular, resulting from strains passed along a series of molecular partners. Could electrostatic discharges be explained similarly? From experiments designed to answer this, he formulated his theory of electricity. He described static discharges as being the result of a release of a strain caused by an electrical force. Currents were made of strains on particles of matter that were passed without any matter itself being transferred.

As he developed his theory of electricity, his mind began to fail him. He suffered memory losses and acted giddy at inappropriate times. Though his wife tried to protect him from embarrassment, by 1840 he could no longer work and did not fully resume his activities until 1844. It is possible that he was suffering from mild chemical poisoning. During this time he was elected an elder of his church, which meant that he preached and helped with the governing of the church. He also rested in Switzerland, where he walked up to 40 miles (64.4 km) a day.

After he resumed his research, he became interested in the relationship between light, electricity, and magnetism. Was there a connection between them? If so, what was the nature of the relationship? He tried many different experiments to determine if there was such a relationship, and his persistence paid off when he placed heavy glass (which, incidentally, he had produced when working on optical glass years before) across the poles of two powerful electromagnets placed side by side. Then he shined *polarized light* (light whose waves are all traveling in the same direction) through the glass at one end. When the magnet was turned on, the direction of the light was rotated. This phenomenon came to be called the Faraday effect. Furthermore, the glass itself was affected. To test this more directly, he hung a bar of heavy glass between the poles of a strong horseshoe-shaped electromagnet, and the glass aligned itself perpendicularly across the lines of force of the magnet. That is, instead of the ends of the bar each reaching toward a magnetic pole, the bar aligned itself transversely between the poles. After further experimentation he found that other substances acted similarly. He called this phenomenon *"diamagnetism"* and concluded that all substances were either magnetic or diamagnetic. These findings earned him the Rumford and the Royal Medals from the Royal Society in 1846.

Though again suffering temporary confusion and memory troubles, in 1846, Faraday published a short paper, "Thoughts on Ray Vibrations." As the title suggests, this paper was simply a series of musings on the subject of *radiation*. In it, he proposed but could not define a relationship between light and magnetism. In 1832, Faraday had deposited an envelope with the Royal Society that clearly stated his belief in the existence of electromagnetic waves, but oddly, this envelope was not opened until 1937.

Throughout the late 1840s and the 1850s, Faraday's skill as a lecturer was perfected. He worked hard to improve his delivery and was very popular among a variety of always crowded audiences. He delighted the attendees with carefully planned experiments and explained the concepts so they could be easily understood. In 1848, he delivered the previously mentioned famous lecture, "The Chemical History of the Candle," and he gave the Christmas lecture every year between 1851 and 1860.

He also continued his research during this time. He was prolific, but his experiments were not as awe-inspiring as his earlier discoveries. He examined the effect of magnetism on gases and found oxygen to be magnetic. He believed in the unity of all natural forces (gravity, light, heat, magnetism, and electricity) and wanted to find a relationship between electricity and gravity but was unsuccessful.

Plain Michael Faraday

In 1857, Faraday was offered the presidency of the Royal Society but declined it. It is said that he feared the effect on his mind of assuming any new responsibilities. He also turned down an offer of knighthood from Queen Victoria, desiring instead to remain plain Michael Faraday. He did accept the offer of a house and garden in Hampton Court by the Queen in 1858. Though his laboratory research had suffered since his breakdown in the early 1840s, he did not resign as a lecturer at the RI until 1861. He was offered the presidency of the RI, but he refused that as well. He did continue advising for Trinity House until 1865, particularly in the matter of electric lighting for the lighthouses. By 1864, he had resigned from all his duties, and he and Sarah moved to their new house permanently in 1865. By the time he died on August 25, 1867, he could barely move or speak. He was buried in the Sandemanian plot in the Highgate Cemetery under a gravestone that, per his request, simply read, "Michael Faraday."

His name lives on. In his honor, a unit of capacitance was named a "farad." The Christmas Lectures that Faraday initiated are now a flagship of the RI and are broadcast internationally. The Institution of Electrical Engineers awards a Faraday medal for notable achievement in the field of electrical engineering and holds annual Faraday Lectures. He was a pure scientist, interested in gaining a better understanding of natural forces but always leaving the applications and widespread fame to others. He was a pioneer who made important foundational discoveries upon which others built new sciences. His achievements were appreciated in his own time; after all, he started so young and accomplished so much. He was honored by over 50 academic societies during his lifetime. Even so, much of the importance of what he discovered was not fully appreciated until the impact of the applications resulting from his research became apparent years later. Faraday never had any formal training. He was particularly deficient in mathematics and relied on others to translate his ideas mathematically into concrete theories, but he had an uncanny sense of the concepts and theories he researched. The application of the phenomena he discovered developed into the modern electrical industry. He deserves remembrance.

CHRONOLOGY

1791	Michael Faraday is born September 22nd in London, England
1805	Becomes an apprentice for Mr. Riebau

1812	Attends scientific lectures given by Sir Humphry Davy
1813	Starts working as a laboratory assistant at the Royal Institution (RI)
1813–15	Tours Europe with the Davys
1815	Starts lecturing at the City Philosophical Society
1815–16	Works on miner's safety lamp with Davy
1816	Becomes lecturer at the RI and publishes first scientific paper on Tuscany limestone
1818–24	Researches steel alloys
1820	Makes first compounds of chlorine and carbon
1821	Devises first electric motor
1823	Produces liquid chlorine
1825	Isolates benzene and becomes director of the laboratory at the RI
1825–29	Works on optical glass quality
1826	Starts Friday Evening Discourses and Christmas Lectures for children
1829–53	Teaches chemistry at the Royal Military Academy
1831	Discovers electromagnetic induction and makes first dynamo
1832	Establishes unity of all types of electricity
1833	Writes the first two laws of electrochemistry
1834	Becomes first Fullerian Professor of Chemistry at the RI
1835	Studies electricity and gases
1836	Becomes scientific advisor to Trinity House
1839	Announces his theory of electricity
1839–55	Publishes three volumes of *Experimental Researches in Electricity*

1845–50	Researches the relationship between electricity, light, and magnetism
1845	Observes rotation of polarized light in magnetic field and diamagnetism
1849	Researches the relationship between electricity and gravity
1859	Publishes collection of his papers, *Experimental Researches in Chemistry and Physics*
1860	Gives famous Christmas lecture, "The Chemical History of a Candle"
1861	Resigns as lecturer at RI
1864	Resigns from all posts
1867	Dies August 25th at age 75

FURTHER READING

Allaby, Michael, and Derek Gjertsen, eds. *Makers of Science*. Vol. 2. New York: Oxford University Press, 2002. Describes the achievements of the world's most famous scientists within their historical contexts. Attractive illustrations.

Heritage Faraday Page. The Royal Institution of Great Britain. Available online. URL: http://www.rigb.org/rimain/heritage/faradaypage.jsp. Accessed on January 28, 2005. Nice biography with lots of photographs and links to other Royal Institution (RI) Web pages.

Meadows, Jack. *The Great Scientists: The Story of Science Told Through the Lives of Twelve Landmark Figures*. New York: Oxford University Press, 1987. Brief biographies of 12 high-profile scientists and the development of science as influenced by social forces. Colorful illustrations.

Saari, Peggy, and Stephen Allison, eds. *Scientists: The Lives and Works of 150 Scientists*. Vol. 1. Detroit, Mich.: U*X*L, 1996. Alphabetically arranged introductions to the contributions of scientists from a variety of fields. Intended for middle school students.

Tyndall, John. *Faraday as a Discoverer.* New York: Crowell, 1961. Memoir of Faraday's life and discoveries written by a personal colleague from the RI.

3

Max Planck

(1858–1947)

Max Planck discovered energy quanta, causing an upheaval in physics.
(© The Nobel Foundation)

The Concept of Quanta of Energy

The observable world normally appears smooth, continuous, and
well-defined. In contrast, the *quantum* world is discontinuous, very
small, random, and abstract. To human eyes, actions in the macroscopic world appear continuous because quanta are so tiny.
Quantum physics is the field that describes behavior and activity at
and below the atomic level. Though the quantum world can be
detected in the lab, quantum changes or actions are too small for

eyes to detect. The concept of energy quanta was discovered by a German physicist at the turn of the 20th century. Max Planck's discovery laid the foundation for quantum theory and revolutionized the field of physics.

Thermodynamics

Max Karl Ernst Ludwig Planck was born to Johann Julius Wilhelm von Planck and Emma Patzig on April 23, 1858, in Kiel, Germany. Johann already had two daughters from his first marriage, and Max was his fourth child from his second marriage. Max began elementary school in Kiel and then continued in Munich at the Königliche Maximilian-Gymnasium in 1867 when his father accepted a position as professor of law at the University of Munich. Max was a talented pianist but reportedly decided against choosing a career in music when he was told by a professional musician that he was not dedicated enough. Nevertheless, Max enjoyed playing the piano throughout his life. When he was in the mood for a more physical activity, he climbed mountains. Max graduated from the Gymnasium in 1874 with very high marks and enrolled at the University of Munich that fall.

At the university, Max began his studies in mathematics but became interested in physics soon afterward. In 1877 and 1878, Max visited the University of Berlin for two semesters. There he was taught by two well-known physicists of the time, Gustav Robert Kirchoff and Hermann Ludwig Ferdinand von Helmholtz. Max independently studied *thermodynamics*, the physics of the relationships between heat and other forms of energy. Energy transformations of all matter are governed by two main laws. The first law of thermodynamics states that energy is conserved; energy can be transferred and transformed, but it can neither be created nor destroyed.

The second law of thermodynamics states that energy transfers or transformations increase *entropy*. Entropy is a measure of disorder, or a measurement of probability of the state of a system. For example, the second law asserts that heat naturally flows from a hot object to a cold object. Just because a process conserves energy does not mean it will occur. Physicists proposed the second law to help predict which processes will occur and which will not. For example, if you put an ice cube into a bowl of hot soup, the heat from the soup will flow to the *molecules* on the ice cube. Energy is transferred from the molecules of the hot soup to the molecules of water in the ice cube. The water molecules begin to move around more, and the ice melts. Energy would still be conserved if heat was transferred from the ice cube to the soup, but an ice cube would never remain frozen when placed into a bowl of hot soup because that would not follow the second law of thermodynamics. Max was attracted to the generality of these principles and chose to write his doctoral dissertation on the second law of thermodynamics. Planck's first major book was an extension of these studies. Published in 1897, *Vorlesungen über Thermodynamik* (Lectures on thermodynamics) included studies of thermodynamic principles and concepts of osmotic pressure, boiling points, and freezing points.

After earning his Ph.D. from the University of Munich in 1879, Planck remained there as a lecturer from 1880 to 1885. The pay was not adequate for him to begin his own family, however, and when a job as associate professor of theoretical physics at the University of Kiel was offered to him, he accepted. With sufficient income to support a family, he married his childhood sweetheart, Marie Merck. They eventually had four children together. By the fall of 1888 Professor Kirchoff had died, and the University of Berlin invited Planck to succeed him. He was appointed assistant professor and the first director of the new Institute for Theoretical Physics in November 1888 and promoted to full professor in 1892. Planck remained at Berlin until he retired in 1926.

The Ultraviolet Catastrophe

While at Berlin, Planck began analyzing *blackbodies*. Blackbodies are theoretical objects that completely absorb all the electromagnetic radiation that falls on them. They also act as perfect radiators, releasing all the radiation in the form of electromagnetic waves. When doing so, the blackbody will no longer appear black because it radiates light, that is, electromagnetic waves in the visible region

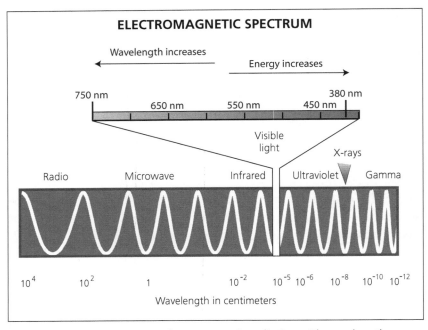

The human eye is sensitive to electromagnetic radiation with wavelengths between 380 and 750 nanometers. The difference between visible light and other forms of electromagnetic radiation is the wavelength.

of the spectrum. For example, as black coals in a barbeque grill heat up, they become red and maybe even orange. As objects become even hotter, they will glow yellowish-white, as the filament of a lighted bulb does. Many wondered why the color changed as the temperature rose. Theorists were having trouble relating the temperature to the emitted radiation spectrum.

Planck investigated the relationship between the electromagnetic energy emitted by blackbodies and varying frequencies and temperatures. The radiation properties of a blackbody depended only on its temperature. At lower temperatures the intensity of the emitted radiation decreased. Less radiation was emitted, but the peak occurred at longer *wavelengths*. Reds occur at longer wavelengths, which is why when an object is initially heated it becomes red. Then as the body grows hotter, the color changes to orange or yellow and eventually to blue (a shift to more energetic, shorter wavelengths of the spectrum). At extremely high temperatures, the blue end of the spectrum is most intense. Thus, as the blackbody absorbs more and more heat, the peak of intensity of the radiation it emits shifts across the electromagnetic spectrum to higher and higher frequencies (i.e., shorter and shorter wavelengths).

All of the above could be determined experimentally and plotted to form a curve, but classical theory could not explain the shape of the curve. There are an *infinite* number of possible frequencies in the high *frequency* range. If, as by definition, a blackbody equally radiated all frequencies of electromagnetic radiation, then most of the energy emitted should be in the high energy region of the spectrum. This corresponds with the very short wavelengths, such as those for ultraviolet waves. However, the empirical curve was not compatible with this prediction. This conundrum was called the ultraviolet catastrophe, and no one could explain it.

For a decade physicists had been trying to explain mathematically how blackbodies radiated heat. A few scientists had come up

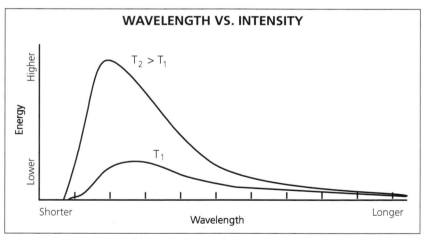

At higher temperatures, the spectral distribution of radiation from blackbodies shifts toward shorter wavelengths (higher frequencies). Note also that the total radiation emitted is greater at higher temperatures.

with seemingly suitable solutions, but their formulations only worked for restricted ranges of wavelengths. German physicist Wilhelm Wien proposed a theoretical curve that worked well for high frequencies. An equation proposed by the English physicist John Rayleigh and modified by the English mathematician and astronomer Sir James Hopwood Jeans accounted for the manner of distribution of low frequencies. Planck became dedicated to reconciling these inconsistencies.

The Quantum Concept

Sticking with a field in which he was comfortable, he attempted to accomplish this by approaching the issue from a thermodynamic perspective. He was unsuccessful for several years, when finally in desperation he made an assumption that led to a lucky breakthrough. He assumed that energy was not infinitely divisible, as are waves, but existed in small specific amounts that he called quanta. German-born physicist Albert Einstein later specifically referred to a quantum of light as a photon. Planck imagined that the size of an energy packet was proportional to its frequency. He was then able to deduce that the energy of an oscillation of a certain frequency equaled the product of that frequency and a constant, which today is referred to as *Planck's constant*. This formula is depicted $E = h\nu$, where E represents the energy emitted, h represents the universal constant, and ν represents the frequency. Planck's constant established the relationship between the energy of an electromagnetic wave and its frequency. Its numerical value equals 6.626×10^{-34} Joule second. Planck's quantum hypothesis thus suggested that the energy of a released photon must be a whole number multiple of $h\nu$.

As mentioned above, to perform the necessary calculations successfully, Planck arbitrarily made the assumption that energy was absorbed and emitted in discrete packages or quantities. At the time, he thought of quanta simply as a mathematical tool to complete the calculations, but it proved to be a revolutionary discovery itself. Eventually it led to the foundation of a new branch of physics—quantum physics, also called *quantum mechanics*. The new concept also solved the problem of the ultraviolet catastrophe.

Blackbodies could easily emit low-frequency, long-wavelength reds since only a small amount of energy would be necessary to form a low-frequency quantum. As temperature increases, more energy is inputted, and higher energy quanta can be radiated. However, at very high frequencies, as in the short wavelength ultraviolet range, it would be difficult to obtain a photon with enough energy to satisfy $E = h\nu$ (since as ν increases, so does E). Since only whole photons can be released, an energy packet of less than h cannot be released. So the abundance of high-frequency emissions predicted by classical physics does not occur.

The concept of quanta was radical because it went against the age-old theme of continuity. Energy was always assumed to be transmitted continuously, like a wave. Actions that can be observed in the macroscopic world and that are described by classical mechanics are continuous. For example, planets orbiting the Sun do not skip between positions; they progress along a continuous pathway. Warmth from an oven does not heat the family room without first gradually warming the kitchen and then traveling to the adjacent room. Despite science fiction fantasies, people cannot be instantaneously beamed from one location to another. The concept of quanta introduced an innovative mechanism of action that has come to describe much of the behavior in the microscopic world, such as that of molecules, atoms, and electrons. Quantum leaps are extremely tiny, as demonstrated by the small value of Planck's constant, thus these discontinuous leaps are not apparent to observers in the macroscopic world.

Planck initially proposed his solution to the blackbody radiation problem during a physics seminar at the University of Berlin in October 1900, but he did not present a theoretical justification of his radiation law until December. The resulting article was published in the *Annalen der Physik* and is one of the most important physics papers of all time. He later admitted that finding the correct formula had been simply lucky guesswork. A fuller account of his ideas was published in his 1906 book, *Theorie der Wärmestrahlung* (*Theory of Heat Radiation*, 1959).

A decade after Planck's discovery of quantum action, the field of physics had fully accepted and begun building upon the revolutionary idea. The application of his serendipitous discovery led to

The Most Coveted Award

For a scientist, receiving a Nobel Prize is the highest honor obtainable. Alfred Bernhard Nobel was a 19th-century inventor born in Stockholm, Sweden, on October 21, 1833. His father was a chemist who helped the Russian army develop naval mines to discourage enemy ships from approaching the firing range of St. Petersburg. As an adult, Nobel also became interested in explosives, particularly the oily, unstable liquid nitroglycerin. He believed it would be useful in construction if it could be made safer somehow. By 1862, he had invented dynamite, an explosive made of nitroglycerin absorbed into a porous material and wrapped into a cylindrical container that also held a primary charge and a fuse, allowing it to be detonated from a distance. Nobel's younger brother was tragically killed in 1864 when nitroglycerin in a Stockholm laboratory accidentally exploded. When a newspaper incorrectly reported that Nobel rather than his brother had died, he realized that the world viewed his achievement as a murderous war weapon. He had intended his invention to serve mankind and decided to set up a foundation with the fortune he earned from dynamite that would honor the achievements of others. In 1900, he bequeathed the equivalent of $9.2 million to establish the Nobel Foundation. Nobel Prizes have been awarded annually since 1901 to living individuals who have made extraordinary contributions to the fields of physics, chemistry, physiology or medicine, literature, and peace. The recipients, called Nobel laureates, receive a gold medal, a personal diploma, and a monetary prize worth more than $1 million. In 1968, the Bank of Sweden established the Prize in Economic Sciences in Memory of Alfred Nobel. Alfred Nobel died from a cerebral hemorrhage on December 10, 1896, at his home in San Remo, Italy.

the resolution of many incongruities between classical theoretical physics and experimental physics. Most notably, Einstein extended Planck's ideas to the wave-particle duality of light, proposing that light was emitted in individual quanta of energy called photons, and Danish physicist Niels Bohr developed the quantum mechanical model of the atom. In 1918, Planck was awarded the Nobel Prize in physics for his discovery of elementary energy quanta. In the 1920s, the new field of quantum mechanics was established. Planck was elected a foreign member of the Royal Society in 1926 and awarded the Copley Medal in 1928.

Personal Tragedies

These scientific achievements and awards could not protect Planck from several personal tragedies during this time. His wife Marie had died in 1909. A daughter died during childbirth in 1917. Two years later, her twin sister, who had married her late sister's husband, died in the same manner. Lastly, one of his sons died on the battlefield during World War I. Planck did remarry in 1911 to his late wife's niece, Marga von Hoessli. Together they had one son.

Most of Planck's achievements following his Nobel-winning science were administrative. Planck did not shy from administrative positions. He felt it was his responsibility as a scientist to promote scientific interests and was instrumental in bringing many talented scientists to Germany. In 1894, he became a member of the Prussian Academy of Sciences, and he served as permanent secretary from 1912 to 1938. He served as editor of *Annalen der Physik*, a physics journal. In 1929, he was awarded what has become the highest distinction bestowed by the German Physical Society, the Max Planck Medal. In 1930, he was appointed president of the Kaiser Wilhelm Society in Berlin. He held this post until 1937, when he was forced to resign after intervening with Adolf Hitler on behalf of his Jewish colleagues. After the war, the society was renamed the Max Planck Society and moved to Göttingen in 1945. Planck served as temporary president during this difficult transitional period until his death in 1947.

Planck did engage in some intellectual pursuits later in his life. He performed research trying to assimilate his quantum concept into Einstein's theory of *relativity*, for which he became a staunch supporter. He also published works concerning his overall philosophy of science. In 1935, he published a book, *Die Physik im Kampf um die Weltanschauung* (Physics in the fight for the world view), which approached general philosophical, religious, and societal issues through the use of physics. Planck was always attracted to generalizations. He relentlessly sought out constants of nature. He believed in the absolute validity of simple and accurate natural laws. These ideas were conveyed in his book, *The Philosophy of Physics* (translated by W. H. Johnson, 1936).

When the Second World War broke out, Planck felt it was his duty to stay in Germany and try to preserve the integrity of scientific research. However, his efforts against the Nazi regime were futile. In 1943, he moved to Rogätz, and in 1945, some American colleagues took him to Göttingen, where he spent the last two years of his life with his grandniece. Sadly, his home had burnt down during an air raid, and he lost most of his research manuscripts and books. In 1944, his surviving son from his first marriage was arrested and executed for conspiring to assassinate Adolf Hitler.

An Honored Physicist

Max Planck passed away on October 3, 1947, at Göttingen. He was a man respected as much for his personal characteristics of integrity and sense of duty as he was for his scientific accomplishments. In his honor the Max Planck Society was founded in 1948 in Göttingen. It is the successor to the Kaiser Wilhelm Society for the Advancement of Science. The society's research institutes perform basic research in the interest of the general public in the natural sciences, life sciences, social sciences, and the humanities, particularly in areas that German universities cannot. In addition, the German Physical Society continues to present the prestigious Max Planck Medal annually to an outstanding theoretical physicist.

Today quantum mechanics explains phenomena such as the spectral distribution of electromagnetic radiation and how atoms combine into molecules. Its applications have led to technological advancements, including bar code readers at the supermarket, lasers, compact discs, and *nuclear energy*. The natural science of physics has been separated into two eras. Classical physics encompasses everything before 1900, pre-quantum theory, such as heat, light, sound, mechanics, and thermodynamics. Modern physics includes everything post-quantum theory, such as relativity, nuclear physics, and big bang cosmology. Planck's constant is found in numerous quantum mechanical formulas and has long been universally accepted, but the concept of quanta is more than a collection of mathematical formulas or the basis of a bunch of modern electronic devices. It explains the fundamental basis of all physical processes.

CHRONOLOGY

1858	Max Planck is born April 23rd in Kiel, Germany
1874–75	Studies at the University of Munich
1877–78	Studies at the University of Berlin
1879	Receives doctoral degree for his dissertation on thermodynamics from the University of Munich and begins lecturing there
1885	Is appointed associate professor at the University of Kiel
1888	Becomes assistant professor at the University of Berlin and director of the Institute for Theoretical Physics
1892	Is promoted to full professor at the University of Berlin
1897	Publishes first major book on thermodynamics (*Vorlesungen über Thermodynamik*)
1900	Proposes the idea of quanta
1906	Publishes the book *Theorie der Wärmestrahlung* (Theory of heat radiation)
1918	Is awarded the Nobel Prize in physics "in recognition of the services he rendered to the advancement of physics by his discovery of energy quanta"

1926	Retires and becomes professor emeritus at the University of Berlin
1929	Receives first Max Planck Medal by the German Physical Society
1930–37	Serves as president of Kaiser Wilhelm Society (now the Max Planck Society)
1944	Home, manuscripts, and books are destroyed in air raid
1947	Dies October 4th in Göttingen, Germany

FURTHER READING

Adler, Robert E. *Science Firsts: From the Creation of Science to the Science of Creation.* New York: John Wiley, 2002. Stories of 35 landmark scientific discoveries, including scientific and historical contexts.

Boorse, Henry A., Lloyd Motz, and Jefferson Hane Weaver. *The Atomic Scientists: A Biographical History.* New York: John Wiley and Sons, 1989. Explains the rise of atomism, with a focus on the personalities involved.

Gamow, George. *The Great Physicists from Galileo to Einstein.* New York: Dover, 1961. Physicist author explains how the central laws of physics were revealed. Includes some biographical data.

Nobelprize.org. "The Nobel Prize in Physics 1918." Available online. URL: http://nobelprize.org/physics/laureates/1918. Last modified on June 16, 2000. Includes biography, Nobel lecture, banquet speech, and links to other references.

Segrè, Emilio. *From X-Rays to Quarks: Modern Physicists and Their Discoveries.* San Francisco, Calif.: W. H. Freeman, 1980. Development of modern physics written by a Nobel laureate.

Simonis, Doris A., ed. *Lives and Legacies: Scientists, Mathematicians, and Inventors.* Phoenix, Ariz.: Oryx Press, 1999. Contains one-page profiles.

4

Ernest Rutherford

(1871–1937)

Ernest Rutherford explained the nature of radioactivity and dissected the structure of the atom. (© The Nobel Foundation)

Discovery of the Atomic Nucleus

Everyone has come into contact with *radioactivity;* it is a natural phenomenon. Since the creation of the universe, atoms have been spraying out radioactivity. Most atomic nuclei are quite stable and will not change even if given one million years. Others are so unstable that they only exist for a few seconds before spontaneously breaking down. Because radioactivity is invisible, intangible, and odorless, people were not aware it existed until the end of the 19th century. Atoms were believed to be the smallest particles that could exist but then, in the 1890s, scientists found atoms that naturally broke down into even smaller subatomic particles. The pioneering physicist Ernest Rutherford explained radioactivity as the product of atomic disintegration and then used it as a tool to probe the structure of the atom. He discovered that elements not only could be transmutated, a feat that alchemists had been trying in vain to accomplish for centuries using chemical means, but also that some elements transform themselves. The Royal Swedish Academy of Sciences awarded Rutherford the Nobel Prize in chemistry in 1908 for his investigations into the disintegration of the elements and the chemistry of radioactive substances.

Son of a Flax Farmer

The fourth of 12 children, Ernest Rutherford was born to James and Martha Thompson Rutherford in the rural village of Spring Grove, New Zealand, near Nelson, on August 30, 1871. His family moved to Pungarehu when he was 15. His father was a wheelwright, a flax farmer, and ran a mill, and his mother was a schoolteacher. Because Ernest was an excellent primary school student, he earned a scholarship to Nelson College, a high school, and then was awarded a scholarship to Canterbury College (now Canterbury University), in Christchurch. After earning a bachelor of arts in 1892, he pursued a master's degree in mathematics and physical science, which he received in 1893 with double first-class honors. One year later, he obtained a bachelor of science degree. He became engaged to Mary Newton, the daughter of his landlord, while he attended Nelson, but he needed a steady job before they could marry. The award of an 1851 Exhibition Science Scholarship allowed him to go to the Cavendish Laboratories at Trinity College at Cambridge University, in England.

A Stimulating Atmosphere

At Canterbury, Rutherford researched the magnetization of iron by using an alternating electric current. He utilized this knowledge to

Pioneers in Radioactivity

Wilhelm Conrad Röntgen (1845–1923) earned the first Nobel Prize in physics for his discovery of X-rays in 1895. As a physics professor at the University of Würzburg, in Germany, Röntgen began studying *cathode rays* in 1894. Cathode rays are invisible streams of electrons that result from the discharge of an electrical current within a vacuum tube. If the glass tube's walls are coated with zinc sulfide, the glass fluoresces when hit by the rays. One day, in order to visualize the greenish fluorescent glow better, Röntgen darkened his lab and wrapped black paper around the vacuum tube. He noticed that a nearby screen coated with barium platinocyanide crystals began to glow. After more experiments, he learned that the radiation could pass through some materials, such as glass, wood, or human flesh, but not others, such as metals, and it exposed a photographic plate. He named these mysterious emanations "X-rays."

French physicist Antoine-Henri Becquerel (1852–1908) won the Nobel Prize in physics in 1903 for his discovery of spontaneous radioactivity. He was interested in luminescence, the property of emitting light. After a conversation with Röntgen, Becquerel wondered if there was a connection between X-rays and phosphorescence. He found that uranium salts, which phosphoresce after exposure to light, darkened a wrapped photographic plate. The uranium rays that penetrated the wrapping to expose the photographic plate also ionized gases, as did X-rays, but were not deflected by electromagnetic fields. He shared his Nobel Prize with Pierre and Marie Curie, who further characterized the phenomenon of radioactivity.

devise a detector for electromagnetic waves using the same principles that Italian inventor Guglielmo Marconi later used in the development of wireless telegraphy. Though the resident scientists at Cavendish typically were hesitant to accept foreigners into their exclusive society, they were impressed by the range and sensitivity of Rutherford's electromagnetic detector. Under the direction of Sir Joseph John Thomson, an expert on electromagnetic radiation, Rutherford became the first research student at the Cavendish Laboratory.

The same year Rutherford arrived at Cambridge, Wilhelm Conrad Röntgen discovered *X-rays*. Then in 1896, Antoine-Henri Becquerel discovered radioactivity. Cambridge University was also emerging as a powerful force in the advancement of physics research. In 1897, Thomson, the director of the Cavendish Laboratory, discovered the electron while researching the behavior of electricity in gases. Rutherford was certainly in the right place at the right time to make a major advancement.

Soon after Thomson suggested Rutherford study X-rays and their effect on gases, Rutherford showed that treatment with X-rays ionized gas molecules. From Rutherford's experiments, Thomson proposed a theory of *ionization*, which stated that X-rays created an equal number of positive and negative *ions*. This eventually became a diagnostic test for the presence of X-rays. In 1897, he began examining uranium rays, discovered by Becquerel. Rutherford wrapped uranium in layers of aluminum foil and examined the ability of the uranium rays to penetrate the foil. He found two different types of radiation emanated from the uranium source, alpha and beta rays. Alpha rays were slower and less penetrating, while beta rays were quicker, more penetrating, and not readily absorbed by the air. Rutherford later determined the nature of *alpha particles*, which consist of two positive charges. Others determined that *beta particles* consist of one negative charge. French scientist Paul Villard is credited with discovering a third type of radiation, gamma radiation, in 1900.

A Productive Partnership

In 1898, Rutherford was offered the Macdonald Professorship of Experimental Physics at McGill University in Montreal, Canada. At McGill he started studying thorium, which was also radioactive, but its emissions seemed irregular compared to those of uranium. Rutherford thought this was due to the release of a radioactive gas that he called thorium emanation. He isolated and identified the gas thoron (now known to be an *isotope* of radon), a member of the family of inert gases. He also figured out that the activity of the emanation decreased with time.

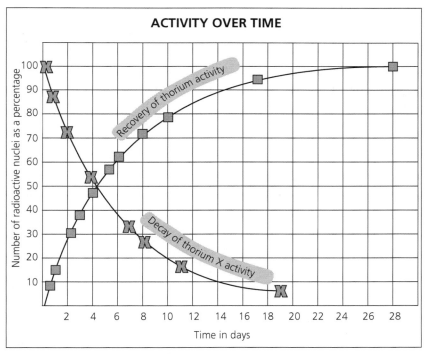

After separation, the radioactivity of the newly created thorium-X decreased as inactive thorium regained its activity.

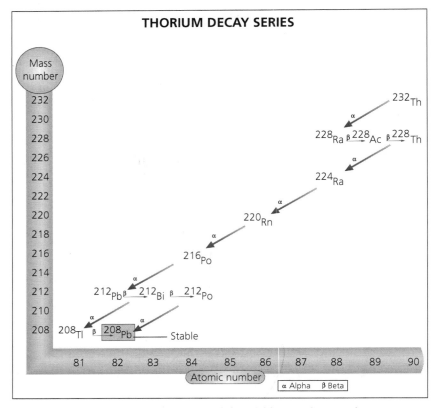

THORIUM DECAY SERIES

As radioactive chemical elements emit alpha and beta radiation, they are transformed into related series of different elements until they reach a stable end product.

Now that Rutherford had a steady job, he married Mary Newton in 1900, and they had one daughter, named Eileen, in 1901.

In 1901, Rutherford teamed with a skilled chemist, Frederick Soddy, who had recently arrived at McGill. Together, they successfully separated the active thorium emanation, which they named thorium-X, from the then inactive thorium compound. They were surprised to find that the activity of thorium-X decreased with time, and the activity of the inert thorium regained its activity within a few weeks. Becquerel had made a similar observation with uranium, which led Rutherford and Soddy to believe it was a real phenomenon. After further investigation, by 1903, Rutherford and Soddy developed the disintegration theory of radioactivity. Thorium atoms were disintegrating into smaller parts, releasing radiation in the process. Thorium-X was one of the breakdown products; when separated from its source, its activity could no longer be replenished by the decaying thorium atoms, so it gradually became inactive. The apparently inactive thorium regained its activity as it spontaneously generated new radioactive products.

Radioactive substances, such as uranium, thorium, and radium, all seemed to follow a specific pathway as they disintegrated. The *decay series* progressed predictably as an atom lost alpha and beta particles until it reached a stable form, that is, a different element that was not radioactive. Each radioactive substance has a unique *half-life*. A half-life of an isotope is the time it takes for half of the original amount of radioactivity in a sample to decay. As a result of alpha decay, the *atomic number* decreases by two and the *atomic weight* decreases by four. In *beta decay*, the atomic number increases by one but the atomic weight stays the same.

Rutherford and Soddy published their conclusions regarding the nature of radioactivity in "The Cause and Nature of Radioactivity," published in two parts in *Philosophical Magazine* (1902). The explanation earned Rutherford election to the Royal Society of London in 1903 and the Nobel Prize in chemistry in 1908. Rutherford knew that matter contained an enormous amount of energy and realized the impact of his discovery. He expressed his wish that scientists would not learn how to release the energy held tightly within the atom until the world first learned how to live in peace. He also had the insight to recognize that natural radioactivity could shed light onto the question of the age of the Earth. By calculating the rate of formation of lead, the stable end product of the thorium decay series, he determined the age of some rock samples to be greater than one billion years. In 1904, he published the book *Radioactivity*, and in 1906, *Radioactive Transformations*.

Frederick Soddy

Frederick Soddy was born in Eastbourne, England, on September 2, 1877. He attended Eastbourne College, then Oxford University. In 1900, he traveled to the University of Toronto upon hearing of a job opening in chemistry. The position had been filled by the time he arrived, and he ended up as a chemistry demonstrator at McGill University in Montreal, where he began collaborating with Ernest Rutherford. Together the two delineated the process of nuclear decay, during which the composition of a radioactive substance is altered.

In 1903, Soddy returned to London and worked at Merton College, Oxford University, with William Ramsay, who discovered noble gases. Together they examined the gaseous emanations from radium and showed that helium was produced during its decay. From 1904 to 1914, Soddy was a lecturer in physical chemistry at the University of Glasgow, in Scotland, and he formulated the displacement law, which stated that the emission of an alpha particle caused a decaying element to move two

Description of the Atom

Though he had a well-equipped laboratory, Rutherford wanted to be closer to the academically rich environment of England. When he was offered a chair as the Langworthy Professor of Physics at the University of Manchester in 1907, Rutherford excitedly accepted. He continued studying radioactivity, surrounded by highly esteemed colleagues and other past and future Nobel laureates.

Rutherford was most interested in the alpha emanations. In 1909, he ascertained that an alpha particle was the equivalent of a helium atom with a double positive charge. This conclusion was confirmed

places back in the periodic table. In 1913, he figured out that sometimes the elements produced within a radioactive decay series were chemically indistinguishable, though they had different atomic weights. He named these different forms of the same element "isotopes."

Soddy was appointed a professor of chemistry at the University of Aberdeen in 1914 and then was a professor of chemistry at Oxford University from 1919 until he retired in 1937.

Soddy earned the Nobel Prize in chemistry in 1921 for his contributions to knowledge of the chemistry of radioactive substances and his investigations into the origin and nature of isotopes. Later in life, Soddy was involved in politics and economics. He died on September 22, 1956, at Brighton.

Frederick Soddy was awarded the Nobel Prize in chemistry in 1921 for making significant contributions to the understanding of radioactivity and the nature of isotopes. (© *The Nobel Foundation*)

spectroscopically. Rutherford and Johannes Hans Wilhelm Geiger, his student assistant, devised a method for counting the number of released alpha particles. Since alpha particles ionized gas, when fired into a vacuum tube containing a single charged wire, an electrometer could detect the magnified charge of a single particle, thus the number of alpha particles emitted per second could be counted directly. Geiger later improved this method to develop a device called the Geiger counter for measuring radiation. Because the alpha particles caused flashes of light called scintillations when they hit a zinc sulfide screen, Rutherford later switched to scintillation counting, which was more consistent.

The avenue that Rutherford's research followed next led to perhaps his most important breakthrough, the discovery of the structure of the atom. Rutherford suggested to Ernest Marsden, an undergraduate student, that he examine the backward scattering of alpha particles from metal foil. When a beam of alpha particles was fired at a detection screen behind a sheet of gold foil, the resulting image on the screen was blurred. Using the methods developed by Geiger, they determined that the majority of the particles passed through the foil, indicating that the atoms comprising the foil were mostly empty space. Yet something about the gold was deflecting the pathway of a tiny percentage of the alpha particles. A small percentage of the alpha particles, in fact, was deflected greater than 90 degrees. Rutherford described this shocking event as the equivalent of "firing a 15-inch shell at a piece of tissue paper and it coming back to hit you." Rutherford surmised that a very high, concentrated charge was required to achieve such a great deflection. These investigations stimulated his thinking about the structure of the atom and led him to conclude that the atom had a tiny *nucleus* at its center, surrounded by orbiting electrons. Previously, the working model for the structure of the atom was suggested by Thomson, and this model suggested that subatomic particles were clustered together in a spherical formation with the electrons embedded in a positively charged cloud like plums in pudding. If this were the true structure, however, the alpha particles aimed at the center would not be deflected as witnessed but would be carried around like comets around the Sun. Rutherford dismissed the "plum pudding" model for a planetary model that was later refined by the Danish physicist Niels Henrik David Bohr. Though improved, Rutherford's model was not perfect, as it had thermodynamic problems. Bohr accounted for these, as well as the quantization hypothesis proposed by Max Karl Ernst Ludwig Planck, in his model that included orbits of specific energies.

During World War I, many of the Rutherford lab members enlisted in the military. Rutherford himself was temporarily sidetracked from his research to lend his expertise to the Admiralty's Board of Invention and Research Committee by researching underwater acoustics for the detection of submarines.

A Deliberate Change

In 1919, Thomson retired as the Cavendish professor of physics, and Rutherford replaced him. The laboratory was very industrious and productive under his leadership. Rutherford continued his research in nuclear physics, working closely with Sir James Chadwick. The nucleus of an atom contains all the positively charged *protons* and the *neutrons*, which are not charged. The nucleus contributes only a tiny amount to the overall size of the atom but contains most of the mass. At the time, the subatomic particles called protons had not yet been discovered. Protons are simply positively charged hydrogen atoms (hydrogen atoms that have lost their electron). They found that they could use alpha particles as bullets to crack open several lighter elements. When Rutherford passed energetic alpha particles through nitrogen gas, protons resulted. He correctly guessed that the protons were expelled from the nuclei of the nitrogen atoms following absorption of an alpha particle, converting nitrogen to an isotope of oxygen. Nitrogen has an atomic number of seven, thus the absorption of an alpha particle (containing two protons) followed by the loss of one proton (the hydrogen) would result in the formation of oxygen, which has an atomic number of eight. This was the first successful, purposeful transmutation of one element into another.

During the period 1925–30, Rutherford served as president of the Royal Society of London. He also served, in 1933, as president of the Academic Assistance Council, which assisted Jewish scientists fleeing Nazi Germany. As director, he was very busy, yet he continued his research. In 1934, with Marcus Oliphant and Paul Hartek, Rutherford performed the first man-made nuclear fusion reaction. He bombarded deuterium, an isotope of hydrogen with a mass of two, with deuterons (the nuclei of deuterium atoms) and produced tritium, the isotope of hydrogen with a mass of three. (Hydrogen has an atomic weight of 1.00.)

Ernest Rutherford died on October 19, 1937, following surgery to correct a long-neglected hernia. His cremated remains were buried in Westminster Abbey. He was awarded over 20 honorary degrees and several medals during his lifetime, including the

Rumford Medal (1905) and the Copley Medal (1922) of the Royal Society. He also served as chairman of the advisory council to the British government's Department of Scientific and Industrial Research. He published several books and many articles, though he never took a break from his research or lecturing to do so. Rutherford was knighted (1914), given the highest civilian honor, the Order of Merit (1925), and elevated to the peerage of the United Kingdom (1931) as Baron Rutherford of Nelson.

Rutherford was an intellectual giant. He was able to synthesize what he saw in the lab and build on the work of his predecessors to advance physics. He was fortunate to have many talented collaborators and insightful colleagues, and under his direction, numerous revolutionary breakthroughs were made. His description of the nature of radioactivity opened doors to a new field of physics research. His discovery and then use of alpha particles as a tool led to the revealing of inner atomic architecture. By successfully inducing disintegration, he performed the first successful transmutation of one element into another and shattered the long-held belief that the atom was indestructible.

Rutherford's favored alpha particles were big, and therefore he was successful in using them to bombard the nuclei of light elements, but they were not energetic enough to break into the nuclei of heavier elements. American physicist Ernest Orlando Lawrence used protons to probe nuclei. They were not as heavy as alpha particles, but he could accelerate them using an electric field in a machine called a *cyclotron*. The increase in force allowed the artificial disintegration of heavier elements that had such a strong positive charge on their nuclei that approaching alpha particles would be repelled. Rutherford witnessed this technological advancement develop during the last five years of his life.

CHRONOLOGY

1871	Ernest Rutherford is born August 30th in Spring Grove, New Zealand (later Brightwater)
1887	Enters Canterbury College in Christchurch, New Zealand

1892	Receives a bachelor of arts degree from Canterbury College
1893	Receives a master of arts degree in mathematics and mathematical physics from Canterbury
1894	Studies the magnetization of iron by electromagnetic radiation and receives a bachelor of science degree from Canterbury College
1895	Receives a scholarship to Trinity College at Cambridge University, in England, and becomes the first research student at the Cavendish Laboratory
1896	Shows that X-rays break gases down into charged ions
1897	Begins studying radioactivity and distinguishes alpha and beta radiation while studying uranium
1898	Is appointed the second Macdonald Professor of Experimental Physics at McGill University, Montreal, Canada
1899	Starts studying thorium and its emanations
1902	Publishes "The Cause and Nature of Radioactivity" in *Philosophical Magazine* with Frederick Soddy
1904	Rutherford publishes *Radioactivity,* which immediately becomes a classic. Advances in the field accumulated so quickly that a second edition had to be published the following year
1906	Publishes *Radioactive Transformations*
1907	Is appointed the Langworthy Professor of Physics at the University of Manchester
1908	Rutherford is awarded the Nobel Prize in chemistry for his investigations into the phenomenon of radioactivity
1909	Describes the nature of the alpha particle as a helium atom with a double positive charge
1911	Discovers the atomic nucleus and proposes his planetary model of the atom

1919	Becomes the Cavendish Professor of Physics at Cambridge and detects protons in the nucleus
1934	Performs the first fusion reaction with Marcus Oliphant and Paul Hartek
1937	Rutherford dies October 19th in Cambridge, England, following surgery and is buried at Westminster Abbey in London

FURTHER READING

"Ernest Rutherford." The Chemical Heritage Foundation, 2000. Available online. URL: http://www.chemheritage.org/EducationalServices/chemach/ans/er.html. Accessed on January 30, 2005. Part of the chemical achievers series that profiles several pioneering chemists. Intended for high school students.

Heilbron, J. L. *Ernest Rutherford and the Explosion of Atoms.* New York: Oxford University Press, 2003. Examines Rutherford's personality and events leading to his major discovery. Intended for young adults.

Magill, Frank N., ed. *Dictionary of World Biography.* Vol. 9. Pasadena, Calif.: Salem Press, 1999. Contains profiles of world-famous people and their life's work, includes bibliographical references.

Olson, Richard, ed. *Biographical Encyclopedia of Scientists.* Vol. 4. New York: Marshall Cavendish, 1998. Clear, concise summary of major events in the scientists' lives, at an accessible level for middle school students.

Nobelprize.org. "The Nobel Prize in Chemistry 1908." Available online. URL: http://nobelprize.org/chemistry/laureates/1908. Last modified on June 16, 2000. Contains links to Rutherford's biography, Nobel lecture, and other resources.

Lise Meitner

(1878–1968)

Lise Meitner, shown here with Otto Hahn, explained the process of nuclear fission. *(Science Photo Library/Photo Researchers, Inc.)*

Nuclear Fission

Many people would give up the opportunity to work in a field if they were forced to endure repeated extreme hardships. A gentle woman born in the 19th century was so captivated by physics that she fought against gender discrimination and racial persecution, worked without pay for many years, and lived in exile to pursue her dream. As a result, she made one of the world's most amazing discoveries in physics, yet the ultimate recognition a physicist could receive for her work, the Nobel Prize, was awarded to someone else. Lise Meitner was an exceptional experimental physicist and a deep thinker who generously offered the scientific establishment the benefits of her brilliant mind. A pioneer in the study of radioactivity, she discovered the element protactinium and interpreted the process of *nuclear fission*, making possible the development of nuclear power and nuclear weapons.

The Struggle to Obtain an Education

Elise Meitner was born to Philipp and Hedwig Skovran Meitner on November 7, 1878, in Vienna, Austria. She was the third of eight children. Her grandparents were all Jewish; however, the family did not practice Judaism. Her father was a prosperous lawyer, one of the first Jewish lawyers in Vienna. Lise enjoyed math and science and was a bright student; unfortunately, girls were only permitted to attend public schools until the age of 14. She enrolled in a teacher's preparatory school and trained to become a French teacher, but Lise was never enthralled with this as a career choice.

Times were beginning to change, and universities across the country were beginning to accept women as students. The opportunity excited Lise, but she had to study hard with a private tutor to pass the entrance examination since she never had the opportunity to take college preparatory courses at a gymnasium. When she was almost 23 years old, she entered the University of Vienna, where she enrolled in heavy course loads of difficult classes, including calculus, chemistry, and physics.

Physics fascinated Lise. All of her physics classes were taught by Professor Ludwig Eduard Boltzmann, who championed educational opportunities for women and introduced her to the atomic theory, which stated that all matter was composed of atoms. After completing her coursework in 1905, Lise performed research on the conduction of heat in solids and passed an oral exam to obtain a doctorate degree in 1906. She was only the second woman in Vienna to receive a physics doctorate.

There were few paying jobs for trained physicists and none for women. Meitner was forced to accept a position teaching at a girls'

Boltzmann's Imprint

Austrian theoretical physicist Ludwig Eduard Boltzmann (February 20, 1844–October 5, 1906) was Meitner's first mentor and imparted upon her a love of physics. But Boltzmann impacted the development of the science of physics in many other ways as well. He was the first to apply mathematics of probability to the molecular state of a system to interpret its entropy. He deduced the Boltzmann equation, which mathematically described the tendency of a system toward disorder. Part of this equation, the Boltzmann constant, relates the average energy of a molecule to its *absolute temperature*. Boltzmann is given joint credit with James Clerk Maxwell for discovering the kinetic theory of gases. Boltzmann also made contributions in the field of radiation. With Austrian physicist Josef Stefan (1835–93), he developed the Stefan-Boltzmann law, which stated that the rate of radiation of energy from an object was proportional to the fourth power of its absolute temperature, its temperature on the Kelvin scale.

For 40 years, Boltzmann struggled to convince the scientific establishment of atomism, the theory that stated that all matter was composed of atoms. Actually, his battles went deeper than that. He also fought for the right to theorize, believing it was scientific and served a useful purpose as a means to approximate unobservable truths. For example, atoms could not be seen, but they were still a significant factor in scientific discussions. Experimentation was important, not to justify knowledge but rather to disprove theories. His opponents, the logical positivists, believed that science should address only that which could be directly observed. They considered only knowledge derived from verifiable sensory data or experimentation legitimate.

school, and in the evenings she did research on radioactivity with Stefan Meyer, who succeeded Boltzmann as director of the Physics Institute at the University of Vienna. Radioactivity had only been discovered a decade before. Meitner measured the absorption of alpha and beta radiation by various metal foils. She used an instrument called a leaf electroscope that consisted of a thin sheet of aluminum or gold attached to a metal rod. When electrically charged, the leaf was repelled from the rod; in the presence of radiation, the surrounding air would become ionized, and the charge in the rod and the leaf would dissipate. The rate at which the leaf returned to its resting position was an indicator of the strength of the radiation. Meitner also performed some of the first experiments showing that alpha rays are scattered as they pass through matter. She showed that as atomic mass increased, so did the degree of scattering.

A Basement in Berlin

Boltzmann always had spoken highly of the research in Berlin, and the equipment used there for studying radioactivity reportedly was much more advanced than in Vienna. Meitner asked her parents for financial support so she could visit there. She went to the University of Berlin, but there she found that Germans discriminated against women more so than in Austria. She had to obtain special permission from the then not-so-open-minded Max Planck to attend his lectures, and she had trouble finding someone who would accept her into their lab to do research. She was fortunate to make the acquaintance of Otto Hahn, a chemist at the Chemistry Institute of Berlin, which was not far from the University of Berlin. He worked on radioactivity and was looking for someone with physics expertise to assist him. The institute's director, Emil Hermann Fischer, allowed Meitner to use an old workshop in the building's basement as her work space. Women were not allowed in the main building, and she had to walk down the street to a nearby restaurant to use the restroom. Two years later, regulations regarding women's education in Berlin were improved and then Fischer warmly welcomed her to the upstairs laboratories and installed a women's restroom.

As radioactive elements disintegrate, or decay, they are transformed into different elements, and in the process, emit radiation. One radioactive form of an element often decays into another isotope that is also radioactive. An isotope is a different form of an element that contains the same number of protons but a different number of neutrons in the nucleus. The atomic number is the same, but the mass is different. The newly created daughter isotope often decays into yet another isotope, and so on. These successive decays are called a series. For years, Meitner and Hahn worked together identifying the elements of radioactive decay series. Chemistry knowledge was necessary to analyze and identify the elements, and physics was required to identify the subatomic particles that were released. One accomplishment during these years was the development of a physical means to separate radioactive parents from their daughter products based on the fact that the daughters recoiled when alpha particles were emitted, as a rifle does when firing a bullet.

In 1912, the Kaiser-Wilhelm Institute (KWI) for Chemistry opened at Dahlem, just outside Berlin, and Hahn joined. (He became its director in 1928.) He asked Meitner to join him there, and she did, though she still received no remuneration for her assistance. Her father had passed away the year before, thus she no longer received the meager living allowance from her family that had carried her through the past few years. Luckily, Planck hired her as his assistant at the University's Institute for Theoretical Physics that same year. As Prussia's first female assistant, her duties were to grade his students' papers. A year later, Fischer appointed her a scientific associate at KWI, the same position held by Hahn, and Hahn and Meitner jointly headed the radioactivity section. Because the building was new, their laboratory was clean of any previous contaminating radioactivity, allowing accurate measurements to be made on weak radioactivities. Meitner made sure the lab stayed that way by placing toilet paper rolls all over the lab for workers to use when handling phones or doorknobs.

When World War I broke out, Meitner served with the Austrian army as an X-ray nurse and assisted in treating wounded soldiers from 1915 to 1917. Hahn also served by helping the Germans to develop poisonous gases to use on their enemies. Meitner returned to Berlin, where she carried on their work, and Hahn joined her in experiments whenever he could take leave.

The Mother Substance and Transuranics

In 1914, the University of Prague offered Meitner a position. She may have been attracted to the better opportunities for advancement, but the offer spurred Fischer to raise her salary to induce her to stay at KWI. In recognition of her brilliance as a physicist, Meitner was put in charge of her own radiophysics department at KWI in 1917 and given another pay increase. Hahn stayed in chemistry.

The element actinium was always found in uranium-bearing minerals, yet clearly was not a daughter of uranium. Together, Hahn and Meitner searched for the parent element of actinium, suspecting there was an intermediate between the two. In 1918, they published their discovery of a new element with atomic number 91, protactinium. The work was published in the *Physical Chemistry Journal* and titled "The Mother Substance of Actinium, a New Radioactive Element of Long Half-Life." Though Meitner did the majority of the work, she listed Hahn as the primary author, giving him the most credit.

Meitner became the first female allowed to lecture at the University of Berlin in 1922. Crowds of reporters came to hear her inaugural lecture titled "The Significance of Radioactivity in Cosmic Processes." The subject matter was reported ignorantly by the press as "cosmetic physics." She was appointed extraordinary professor at the University of Berlin in 1926 but was forced out of this position when Adolf Hitler came to power. She won a silver Leibniz Prize Medal in 1924 from the Berlin Academy of Sciences and the Ignaz Lieben Prize in 1925 from the Vienna Academy of Sciences. As a team, she and Hahn were nominated for the Nobel Prize in chemistry almost yearly from 1924 to the mid-1930s. Independently, she researched the nature of beta rays. She demonstrated that during radioactive decay, the radiation followed the emission of particles rather than acted as a catalyst for it. After the neutron was discovered in 1932, she spent much time researching these nuclear particles.

In 1934, with Hahn and another chemist named Fritz Strassmann, Meitner began studying the radioactive products that resulted from the bombardment of uranium with neutrons. Called *transuranics*, Enrico Fermi had predicted the formation of these elements that were presumed to be heavier than uranium. Hahn went to work trying to isolate and identify these new elements, while Meitner investigated their radioactive nature. Others were also researching transuranics. In Paris, Irène Joliot-Curie reported finding a transuranic with a half-life of three and one-half hours and chemical characteristics similar to thorium (atomic number 90). This suggested that uranium was emitting alpha particles, which Meitner thought unlikely. Joliot-Curie later changed her statement, saying the new element was more similar to the element lanthanum (atomic number 57). Hahn and Strassmann, meanwhile, were furiously trying to identify several other products with curious chemical properties.

The Impossible Conjecture

Outside the research facility, the world was undergoing massive political upheaval. In 1933, Hitler became chancellor of Germany. Nazism robbed Jews of their rights and their dignity. Though she had a Jewish background, Meitner was protected since she had retained her Austrian citizenship, but Germany annexed Austria in 1938, making it a province of Germany. Once Austria no longer existed, Meitner's passport was no longer valid, and Nazi policies impeded her ability to work and travel. At the age of 60, she was forced to flee the country that she had called home for over 30 years.

An acquaintance from the University of Gröningen, the Dutch physicist Dirk Coster, made arrangements, donated his own money, and solicited support from others to help Meitner escape. On July 13, 1938, she illegally crossed the border into Holland and was free. She then traveled to Copenhagen, where she stayed with Niels Bohr and his wife. Her nephew, Otto Robert Frisch, worked for Bohr, but she wanted to go to Sweden, where she was given a position at the Nobel Institute for Experimental Physics in Stockholm, where she worked with the Nobel Prize–winning Swedish physicist Karl Manne Georg Siegbahn.

Meitner lived in meager conditions with her few personal belongings. Months passed before Hahn could send her even a few items of clothing by mail. She maintained an intense correspondence with Hahn regarding the experiments that commenced shortly before her sudden departure. One day in late 1938, Meitner's nephew came to visit her. Meitner shared with Frisch a puzzling result obtained by Hahn and Strassmann. They reported

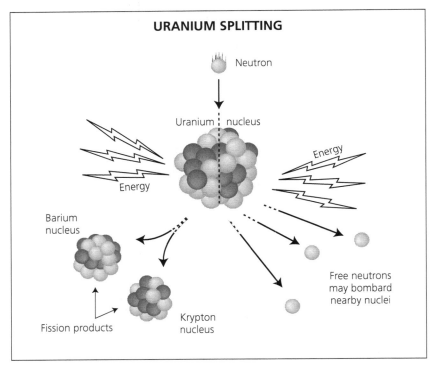

URANIUM SPLITTING

Neutron

Uranium nucleus

Energy

Energy

Barium nucleus

Free neutrons may bombard nearby nuclei

Fission products

Krypton nucleus

Meitner proposed that when uranium was bombarded with neutrons, uranium atoms split into two smaller elements. Shown here, the fission products are barium and krypton, though other products may result. In addition, three neutrons and an enormous amount of energy are released during the process.

obtaining radium isotopes from neutron bombardment of uranium. Meitner could not believe this and asked them to repeat the experiments to be absolutely certain. When they did, they found that, actually, the products were similar to radium but chemically inseparable from barium. They were sure of it; barium was a product of bombarding uranium. But barium had an atomic number of 56, while uranium's was 92, so it could not be a decay product. Where did the barium come from? Meitner suspected that the uranium split into barium and gaseous krypton, which had an atomic number of 36. This would account for all the protons (56 + 36 = 92) but was unheard of. Atoms splitting? Though it may have seemed impossible, her mathematical calculations proved it feasible.

Hahn and Strassmann quickly submitted a paper announcing they had somehow changed uranium into barium. A few weeks later, Meitner and Frisch published the article "Disintegration of Uranium by Neutrons: A New Type of Nuclear Reaction" in the British scientific journal *Nature*, explaining what they termed *nuclear fission*. When a uranium nucleus was bombarded with a neutron, it split into two smaller products, such as barium and krypton. Three neutrons were released, which could subsequently bombard more uranium atoms, causing a chain reaction. Meitner calculated that an enormous amount of energy (200 million electron volts) was released when a uranium nucleus split.

Fallout

The discovery of nuclear fission, or nuclear splitting, made possible the creation of the atomic bomb. When atomic bombs were dropped on Hiroshima and Nagasaki in August 1945, Meitner was devastated. She never intended nor predicted that her research would result in the creation of such a destructive weapon. Reporters swarmed her apartment, and though she vehemently denied any involvement with the design or construction of the bombs, printed articles purported Meitner had a covert role in the development of the bomb. One ridiculous report claimed that she secretly carried the bomb out of Germany in her purse!

In 1944, Otto Hahn alone was awarded the Nobel Prize in chemistry for his discovery of the fission of heavy nuclei. Due to the ongoing war, he did not officially receive his award until 1946.

For a period after the discovery of nuclear fission, it was prudent for Hahn to deny his collaboration with Meitner. It would have endangered his job and possibly his life. But for the rest of his life, he continued to deny her contribution in the discovery of nuclear fission. When he mentioned her at all, it was as his laboratory assistant. This was ludicrous, as she had been named head of the department of radiophysics at KWI back in 1917, and even Strassmann admitted that she had always been the team's intellectual leader. Meitner wondered if Hahn had claimed credit for the discovery so often that he truly began to believe it himself. They had been through too much together for her to cut off contact with him altogether, but his denial hurt and upset her. She agreed that Hahn deserved a Nobel Prize, but felt that she and Strassmann did as well.

Due Recognition

Meitner was invited as a visiting professor to Catholic University in Washington, D.C., in 1946. Her visit was celebrated by Americans who bestowed her with numerous honorary degrees, named her "Woman of the Year," and sat her at the right hand of President Harry Truman to receive an inscribed silver bowl. When she returned to Stockholm, she retired from the Nobel Institute and went to work at the Royal Institute of Technology. The following year, she was given the Max Planck Medal alongside Hahn and Strassmann. This award was especially meaningful, as she greatly admired Planck and had developed a warm friendship with the renowned physicist. In 1966, the U.S. Atomic Energy Commission gave the Enrico Fermi Medal to the trio. This event marked the first non-Americans and the first female recipient of the Fermi award. Meitner's health was failing by then, and she was not able to travel to accept it. She now lived with her nephew in Cambridge, England. She had a heart attack in 1960 and then in 1967 suffered a series of small strokes that left her unable to speak clearly. She died peacefully in her sleep on October 27, 1968, just two weeks shy of her 90th birthday. As she desired, the burial service was small and private. Frisch had her gravestone aptly inscribed, "A physicist who never lost her humanity."

Lise Meitner's physics was of the highest caliber, and fittingly, she was elected to numerous academic organizations, including the Royal Society of London (1955) and the American Academy of Arts and Sciences (1960). She published over 150 scientific articles. Her numerous awards must have brought her some pleasure, but Meitner was driven by her pure desire to understand the physical environment of the world. By doing what she loved, she discovered a new element and discovered and explained the process of atomic fission. She never gave up though she faced many obstacles, such as the struggle to obtain a university education as a woman, the utter impossibility of finding a paid position in the field in which she was trained, the discrimination while trying to make a name for herself in a man's scientific society, the deplorable treatment she endured due to her Jewish ancestry, and most difficult of all, the inconsideration of her closest friend and colleague when she deserved his praise and gratitude. Yet Meitner never publicly complained about not receiving a Nobel Prize or condescended to name-calling. Instead, she spent her life and her energy enjoying her friends and family, and most of all, enjoying the pursuit of knowledge of the natural world.

In 1982, physicists at the Heavy Ion Research Laboratory in Darmstadt, Germany, artificially created an element with atomic number 109 by bombarding bismuth-209 with iron-58. They named it meitnerium.

CHRONOLOGY

1878	Lise Meitner is born November 7th in Vienna, Austria
1901	Enters the University of Vienna
1906	Receives a doctorate degree in physics from the University of Vienna

1907	Moves to Berlin, Germany, and begins working with Otto Hahn at the Chemical Institute of Berlin
1912	Meitner starts working at KWI in Dahlem, Germany, and also is hired as a paid assistant to Max Planck at the university's Institute for Theoretical Physics.
1913	Becomes an associate at KWI, and the joint Laboratorium Hahn-Meitner is founded
1915–17	Serves in World War I as an X-ray nurse for the Austrian army
1917	Becomes head of the new department of radiophysics at the KWI
1918	Meitner and Hahn discover the mother substance of actinium, a rare radioactive element they named protactinium, atomic number 91
1922	Becomes the first female lecturer at the University of Berlin
1926	Is promoted to extraordinary professor at the University of Berlin
1934	Meitner, Hahn, and Fritz Strassmann begin bombarding uranium with neutrons and examining the products
1938	Meitner immigrates to Sweden to escape Nazi Germany and starts working at the Nobel Institute for Experimental Physics in Stockholm
1939	Meitner and her nephew Otto Robert Frisch publish a landmark article, "Disintegration of Uranium by Neutrons: A New Type of Nuclear Reaction," in *Nature* describing nuclear fission
1943	Refuses an invitation from the United States to help build an atomic bomb
1944	Hahn is secretly named the recipient for the Nobel Prize in chemistry for the discovery of nuclear fission
1946	Meitner is a visiting professor at Catholic University, Washington, D.C.

1947	Retires from the Nobel Institute in Stockholm and joins Sweden's Royal Institute of Technology
1953	Retires from Sweden's Royal Institute of Technology at age 75
1968	Dies in her sleep on October 27th at Cambridge, England
1982	Element 109 is artificially created and named meitnerium in her honor

FURTHER READING

Barron, Rachel Stiffler. *Lise Meitner: Discoverer of Nuclear Fission.* Greensboro, N.C.: Morgan Reynolds, 2000. A wonderful, easy-to-read source about Meitner's life and personal struggle to overcome discrimination against her ethnicity and gender to become a pioneer in nuclear physics.

Biographical Memoirs of Fellows of the Royal Society. Vol. 16. London: The Royal Society, 1970. Authoritative, full memoir written by her nephew and collaborator, Otto Robert Frisch. Includes a complete bibliography.

Chemical Heritage Foundation. "Otto Hahn, Lise Meitner, and Fritz Strassmann." Available online. URL: http://www. chemheritage.org/educationalservices/chemach/ans/hms.html. Accessed on January 30, 2005. Part of the chemical achievers biographical profile series aimed at middle and high school students.

Lise Meitner Online. Available online. URL: http://www.users. bigpond.com/Sinclair/fission/LiseMeitner.html. Accessed on November 22, 2004. Contains links to information on the life and work of Meitner, with a tutorial on nuclear fission.

McGrayne, Sharon Bertsch. *Nobel Prize Women in Science.* Washington, D.C.: Joseph Henry Press, 1998. Examines the lives and achievements of 15 women who either won a Nobel Prize, or, like Meitner, played a crucial role in a Nobel Prize–winning project.

Rife, Patricia. *Lise Meitner and the Dawn of the Nuclear Age.* Boston, Mass.: Birkhäuser, 1999. Describes the fascinating life of Meitner and the drama surrounding the discovery of nuclear fission.

Sime, Ruth Lewis. *Lise Meitner: A Life in Physics.* Berkeley: University of California Press, 1996. Complete, in-depth biography, intended for adult readers. Researched from Meitner's personal papers and correspondence. Includes extensive notes.

Albert Einstein

6

(1879–1955)

Albert Einstein possessed possibly the greatest scientific mind of all time. (© *The Nobel Foundation*)

The Theory of Relativity

The name Einstein is synonymous with genius. During the early 20th century, the German-born theoretical physicist Albert Einstein completely transformed the way physicists viewed the universe. He is most famous for developing the theory of relativity, including the famous equation $E = mc^2$, but was awarded the Nobel Prize in physics in 1921 for his research on the *photoelectric effect*. He has been called the greatest scientific mind since Sir Isaac Newton and perhaps of all time.

A Slow Start

Albert Einstein was born on March 14, 1879, to Hermann and Pauline Koch Einstein in Ulm, Germany. The family moved to Munich in 1880, where his father opened an electrical equipment business. They lived in a large house shared with Hermann's brother Jakob, who often brought home science and mathematics textbooks for young Albert. Although Albert did not speak at all until age three and then took six years to become fluent in his own language, he was not a slow learner. The Einstein family was Jewish but not religious, and Albert was enrolled at a Catholic school when he turned five. When he was 10 years old, he started attending another school called the Luitpold Gymnasium. He disliked the strictness and rigidity of the school systems but performed satisfactorily in school due to his independent reading. A medical student who often came to dinner brought Albert books and discussed scientific ideas with him. Albert also learned to play the violin and for the rest of his life enjoyed music as a refuge.

When the business in Munich failed in 1894, the family moved to Milan, Italy, then Pavia. Albert remained in Munich to finish school, but he ended up quitting. Reports claim that he either had or faked a nervous breakdown, and when informing the principal that he was leaving, Albert was told he was expelled for being disruptive. Whatever the reason, he left without a degree. After leaving, he renounced his citizenship so he could later return to Germany without being arrested for dodging the draft. He joined his family and spent the next year writing a paper about the relationship between electricity and magnetism and the ether. The ether was believed to be a medium through which electromagnetic waves were transmitted.

Einstein began studying for the entrance examination to the Swiss Federal Polytechnic Institute in Zurich, perhaps the finest technical school in Europe at the time. His first effort overall was unsuccessful, but his mathematics and physics scores were impressive. Einstein enrolled at the nearby Aarau cantonal school and entered the Polytechnic the following year. His father wanted him to enroll in the engineering program so he would be useful to the family business; however, Einstein decided to enter the general scientific section. Einstein enjoyed tinkering in the physics laboratory but was not favored by his instructors. He often skipped lectures, and when he did attend, he was bored and disruptive. He made friends among his classmates, who happily shared their lecture notes with him, so he managed to pass, but without receiving any recommendations for postgraduate assistantships.

When he graduated in 1900, he was certified as a secondary school teacher and independently performed theoretical research for a doctorate in physics. He became a Swiss citizen, worked as a private tutor, and held a series of temporary teaching positions. He desired a permanent position, since he wanted to marry a Serbian physics student, Mileva Maríc, whom he met while at Polytechnic. In 1902, she gave birth to his daughter Lieserl, whom her parents forced her to give up for adoption. That same year, Einstein was offered a position at the Swiss federal patent office in Bern. His responsibility was to review patent applications for newly invented electrical machines. With a secure job, Einstein married Mileva in 1903 and later had two more children, Hans Albert in 1904 and Eduard in 1910.

His job in the patent office provided Einstein with access to the scientific library and left him plenty of time to think. During his employ, he obtained a doctorate degree in physics from the University of Zurich. His dissertation, published in the *Annals of Physics* in 1905, was titled "A New Determination of the Size of Molecules" and demonstrated a method for determining the size of a sugar molecule. In 1906, he was promoted to the position of technical expert at the patent office.

The Dual Nature of Light

His doctoral dissertation was actually the second of several articles published by Einstein in 1905. This was the year he transformed physics by publishing a series of landmark articles in the *Annals of Physics* that suggested an alternative structure to the foundations of physics. The first paper described the nature of light as both wave-like and particle-like.

In the 17th century, the Dutch physicist Christiaan Huygens first suggested that light was made up of waves and that the waves traveled through a weightless atmospheric medium that he called "ether." In 1704, the English mathematician Sir Isaac Newton published *Opticks*, in which he proposed a corpuscular theory of light. Then, research done by the Scottish physicist James Clerk Maxwell in the mid-1800s and the German physicist Heinrich Rudolph Hertz in the late 1800s further advanced the wave theory of light. Yet no evidence of ether had ever been found, and the wave theory depended upon it since waves required a medium through which they could be transmitted. In 1887, the Americans Albert Michelson and Edward Morley performed experiments that disproved the existence of ether, and then evidence contradicting the wave theory of light came out. Confused physicists could not explain what light actually was. The German physicist Max Planck discovered that light was emitted in packets of specific amounts, called quanta, which led to his quantum theory in 1900. He related the size of the quanta to the frequency of the wavelength of the light.

Einstein used Planck's quantum theory to explain the photoelectric effect, the release of electrons by the atoms of a metal when bombarded with light. Brighter lights brought about the emission of more electrons, but the emitted electrons were not any more energetic, as classical physics predicted. If light with a higher frequency (and therefore shorter wavelength) was shined on the metal, higher energy electrons were released. Einstein explained that if light itself were packaged into discrete quantities (later called photons), as suggested by Planck, then the effect could be explained. Einstein's paper, "On a Heuristic Viewpoint Concerning the Production and Transformation of Light," mathematically demonstrated that light could be treated as both a wave and a particle. A certain color of light had both a specific, measurable wavelength and a definite bundle of energy. Since light was particle-like, it did not require ether to travel. Many scientists had trouble appreciating Einstein's theory until Planck's quantum theory became more widely accepted. For his work explaining the photoelectric effect, Einstein was granted the Nobel Prize in physics for 1921.

Brownian Motion

The third paper Einstein published in 1905, "On the Motion of Small Particles Suspended in a Stationary Liquid, according to the Molecular Kinetic Theory of Heat," also appeared in the *Annals of Physics*. In 1828, the Scottish botanist Robert Brown had described an erratic motion by pollen grains suspended in water. At first he

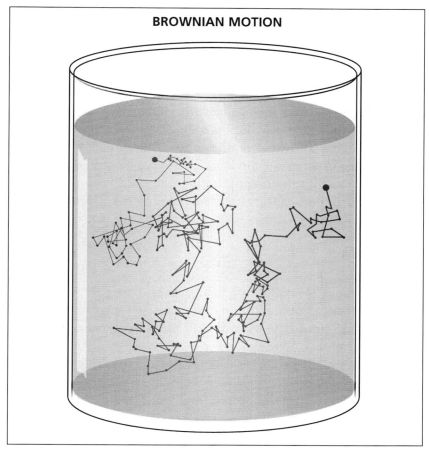

BROWNIAN MOTION

The random, jerky movements of particles suspended in liquids are due to the bombardment of the particles by molecules of the liquid.

thought this jerky activity, later called Brownian motion, was due to a life force inside the pollen grains, but he observed the same motion in nonliving materials such as dye particles. For many decades, no scientist could explain this seemingly perpetual movement, and then Einstein came along and not only explained the movement but used this discovery to prove the existence of molecules. He suggested that an object suspended in a liquid would constantly be bombarded from all directions by molecules of the liquid. Though larger objects would not be moved, smaller objects, such as pollen grains, would be slightly displaced by the force of the impact if hit by more molecules on one side than the opposite. This would make the suspended object appear to be jerking back and forth in a random fashion, just as described by Brown. Since increasingly larger molecules could cause even bigger particles to move by bumping into them, Einstein came up with a way to estimate the average size of the molecules based on the observable effects. Einstein also used mathematical calculations to approximate the amount of molecules in a certain volume of a liquid or gas. A few years after Einstein's publication, the French physicist Jean-Baptiste Perrin performed experiments validating Einstein's theoretical calculations and physically proved the existence of atoms.

Everything Is Relative

As if describing the nature of light and proving the existence of atoms were not enough, Einstein next combined these ideas to form an Earth-shattering theory in his fourth paper of 1905, "On the Electrodynamics of Moving Bodies." He began to doubt how one could know anything to be certain. The idea of possibly not knowing anything plunged Einstein into a virtual cerebral panic. On the verge of eventual mental collapse, one night his special theory of relativity came to him. He proposed that concepts of space and time were only valid in relation to our experiences. In other words, people could know things compared to, or relative to, other things.

In the 17th century, Newton had assumed space and time to be absolute, immovable reference frames. A reference frame describes an observer's position and *velocity* while observing an event. For example, a person sitting inside an airplane, watching the flight attendant roll the service cart down the aisle would consider himself or herself to be sitting still and be able to measure how fast the cart was moving down the aisle toward their seat. However, a person on the ground might be watching the plane fly overhead, and she would consider the plane itself and everything on it to be moving (including the first person that is sitting "still" in their seat). The reference frame to determine how fast the plane was traveling would be how quickly it passed over the observing woman's "unmoving" body. Yet from outer space, the woman herself would appear to be moving, as the Earth on which the woman was standing would be rotating on its axis and also orbiting the Sun. As far as Newton was concerned, space was the immovable reference frame from which all motion ultimately could be measured. This manner of thinking remains suitable for most calculations and viewpoints, but it caused problems when measuring the speed of light.

Would calculation of the speed of light be affected if the person observing the light were moving or if the light source were moving? In 1887, Albert Michelson and Edward Morley were attempting to determine the speed of the rotation of the Earth. In simple terms, they intended to accomplish this by measuring the speed of light in the direction of the rotation of the Earth and at a right angle to the Earth and comparing the differences. Surprisingly, the results for the velocity of light appeared the same in both directions. Because of the Michelson-Morley experiments, Einstein proposed the velocity of light in a vacuum to be constant, independent of the motion of its source. Also, believing that light could travel in a particle-like fashion, and therefore not require ether, he dismissed the ether as superfluous. Without ether, there was no absolute space; there was nothing to serve as an immovable reference frame, and thus, all motion could only be described relative to a particular frame of reference. At this stage, Einstein only considered uniform, nonaccelerated motion, which is why this theory is called the "special" theory of relativity.

The Experiment That Failed

When Einstein proposed his theory of relativity, he set aside Newton's notion of absolute space and time. Einstein assumed the velocity of light in a vacuum to be an unvarying constant and thought light traveled as particles that did not require ether for transmission. Thus its existence was irrelevant, but did it even exist? In 1887, two American scientists set out to verify its existence and ended up doing the opposite.

In 1879, American Albert Michelson had determined the speed of light to be 186,350 miles (300,000 km) per second. With Edward Morley, he next set out to determine the speed of the Earth's wind, the wind created by the Earth's movement through the motionless ether (similar to the breeze created by a speeding car). Prevailing theories held that the ether was a motionless absolute reference frame from which the motion of celestial bodies could be measured. From an observer on the

This assumption that all motion was relative led to the conclusion that time also is relative. Einstein determined that as one approached the speed of light, time would slow down. This thought occurred to him as he was riding in a street car looking back at a clock tower. If he were traveling at the speed of light, the clock hands would appear to be standing still, but the watch in his pocket would continue to advance (though more slowly). For objects traveling at very fast speeds, time advances more slowly. Like space, time also differed depending on the observer's reference frame; time was relative, and time was fused with space. One could not refer to "now" without also referring to "here." Both time and space were necessary to establish a frame of reference.

rotating Earth, the ether would appear to be moving. By measuring the relative speed at which the Earth passed through the ether, the existence of ether could be verified.

Michelson and Morley planned to do this by measuring the speed of light traveling upwind (parallel to the motion of the Earth around the Sun) and comparing it to the speed of light traveling in a different direction (perpendicular to the motion of the Earth around the Sun); the difference between the two would allow calculation of the apparent speed of the ether. This would be similar to measuring the speed of a rowboat traveling with the current and across the current and using the two measurements to calculate the speed of the current. They expected the speed of light to be greater when traveling parallel to the direction of the motion of the Earth than when traveling perpendicular to it, just as traveling with the current would increase the speed of a rowboat. Michelson and Morley sent out light in the direction of the Earth's rotation and at right angles to it. However, when they measured the speed of the light, it was the same in any direction. Thus, the long-assumed ether was only imaginary.

Special relativity changed many previously accepted aspects of physics. One sensational realization was that light was massless energy. The mass of an object would increase as its speed approached the speed of light and, as a result, would require more energy to move it. Photons, particles of light, had eliminated all of their mass and traveled as packets of pure energy. Einstein defined this newly recognized relationship between mass, energy, and the speed of light in the world's most famous equation, $E = mc^2$. (E represents energy, m represents mass, and c is the speed of light.) The major implication of this equation is that matter is simply compressed energy. Mass can be converted to energy, and a miniscule amount of mass possesses a huge amount of energy. The efficiency of nuclear power and the destructiveness of nuclear weapons are based on this principle.

It took time for people to understand Einstein's theory. In 1908, one of his former teachers at the institute, Hermann Minkowski, presented Einstein's theory of relativity and the new concept of fused space-time. Though the faculty at the University of Bern initially had rejected Einstein for a job after he submitted a copy of his theory of relativity in 1907, Minkowski's explanation of the space-time continuum helped the world understand and appreciate the brilliance.

More Generally

The next several years were characterized by a series of academic positions of increasing prestige. In 1908, Einstein was named a privatdozent, an unpaid lecturer, at the University of Bern. The following year, he was appointed associate professor at the University of Zurich. In 1911, he became a full professor at the German University of Prague. During the period 1914–33, Einstein headed the Kaiser Wilhelm Physical Institute in Berlin, became a professor at the University of Berlin, and became a member of the Berlin Academy of Sciences.

Since proposing his special theory of relativity, Einstein had been contemplating the situation of moving bodies in relation to other moving bodies. He published his general theory of relativity "The Foundation of the General Theory of Relativity," in the *Annals of Physics* in 1916. Newton's universal law of gravitation explained many physical phenomena, but discrepancies appeared at the cosmological level. Einstein's general theory of relativity resolved these discrepancies and lifted the restrictions to uniformly moving reference frames from his special theory of relativity.

A significant factor in the general theory of relativity was the principle of equivalence, which stated that no one can determine by experiment if he or she is accelerating or is in a gravitational field. This principle can be illustrated by one of Einstein's famous thought experiments, situations that he contemplated to provide support for or to refute a theory. For example, if a woman in a free-falling elevator were holding a ball, and she let go of it, the ball would not fall to the floor but would appear to float in the air at the same position where her hand let go of the ball. This is true because the elevator would be pulled toward the Earth at the same rate the ball would. If the woman was in an elevator in outer space, away from any gravitational field, and she let go of her ball, it would float, just as if she were in the free-falling elevator. However, if the elevator was ascending, the ball would drop toward the floor when she let go. She would not be able to distinguish whether the ball fell because the elevator was ascending in the absence of gravity or if gravity pulled the ball downward in the absence of ascension. In other words, there is no physical difference between an accelerating frame of reference (the ball falls because the elevator is ascending) and one in a gravitational field (the elevator is at rest, and the ball is pulled downward by gravity).

Whereas Newton's universal law of gravitation described gravity as a force that acted between bodies, Einstein described gravity as a field of curved space surrounding a body; in other words, gravity bent space. Einstein's general theory of relativity predicted that a beam of light, acting like a particle, would bend when passing through a gravitational field. Since light travels faster than anything else, and since it travels the shortest distance between two points, then the shortest distance between two points may be curved rather than straight. Since light traveled at the ultimate speed, then time could not travel faster than light, it would also travel in a curved fashion.

To illustrate the concept of curved space-time, consider a rubber sheet stretched over the edges of a bowl. A marble-size ball, representing light, could roll across the rubber sheet in a straight line. If a weight representing the Sun were placed in the middle of the rubber sheet, it would distort space-time, represented by the rubber sheet. As the marble rolled by the weight, it would follow a curved pathway. Likewise, as light passed by the Sun, the beam would be bent.

Einstein's theory seemed to explain the unusual orbit of Mercury, the planet closet to the Sun, and therefore the most

CURVED SPACE

Large gravitational mass curves the space around it.

Smaller masses and bent light travel through curved space.

The general theory of relativity states that gravity bends space, affecting the motion of objects through space.

affected by the gravitational field surrounding the Sun, but additional practical proof in support of the general relativity theory was not provided until 1919. By then, Einstein's body was worn out. He spent more time theorizing than caring for his own physical needs. He moved in with his cousin Elsa, who cared for him. After he divorced his first wife, he married Elsa.

In November 1919, proof for general relativity was presented by the astrophysicist Sir Arthur Stanley Eddington to a joint meeting of the Royal Society and the Royal Astronomical Society. Eddington had taken photographs of the solar eclipse from the Island of Príncipe in the Gulf of Guinea, off the west coast of Africa. Stars that had not been visible in the presence of sunlight were visible during the total eclipse of the Sun. The positions of the stars during the eclipse were compared with their positions in photographs taken from the exact same location six months before,

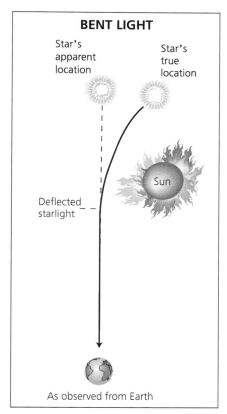

BENT LIGHT

Star's apparent location

Star's true location

Sun

Deflected starlight

As observed from Earth

Einstein's general theory of relativity predicted that starlight would be bent as it passed through the Sun's gravitational field.

when the Sun was on the other side of the world. It appeared as if the stars had moved! Of course, what really happened was that the light from the stars was bent as it passed by the Sun . . . in curved space! Einstein was thrilled that his predictions proved true, and the eccentric, scruffy-looking professor suddenly enjoyed fame among the general public as well as his colleagues.

Grand Unification Failure

For the next 30 years, Einstein struggled unsuccessfully to uncover a grand unified *field theory* that would embrace all of nature's forces, including electromagnetism and gravity. He wanted to find a law that would describe the behavior of everything in the universe, from the elementary particles of an atom to the celestial bodies in the cosmos. He published the first version of his efforts toward this goal in 1929. Some of his colleagues thought he was wasting his time. His most notable accomplishments during the last half of his life were more social and political than scientific. He used his celebrity status to speak out against anti-Semitism, and the Nazis put out a reward for his assassination. In 1933, he left Europe for New Jersey, where he accepted a position at the newly founded Institute for Advanced Study. He became a U.S. citizen in 1940.

In 1939, the Danish physicist Niels Bohr informed Einstein that the German scientists Otto Hahn and Lise Meitner had accomplished nuclear fission and described the enormous power released in the process. Ironically, this phenomenon was predicted in the relationship $E = mc^2$, defined decades before by Einstein himself. Worried about the possible consequences if the Nazis came into possession of nuclear weapons, Einstein wrote a letter to President Roosevelt warning him of the possibilities and destructive power which might soon be in the hands of the Axis. As a result, Roosevelt initiated the top secret Manhattan Project to build the atomic bombs that were ultimately used to end World War II. Einstein later admitted regret for his involvement and spent years after the war campaigning for nuclear disarmament.

In 1952, Einstein was offered the presidency of the new state of Israel. He declined and continued working on his fruitless calculations for a unified field theory. He died at the age of 76 in Princeton, New Jersey, of a ruptured aorta. His body was cremated and his ashes scattered in an undisclosed location.

The results of Einstein's research caused an upheaval in physics. While his work explained some phenomena and results that had puzzled physicists previously, it also forced scientists to abandon what had seemed like common sensical knowledge. The photoelectric effect has been applied in technology such as motion and light sensors and exposure meters on cameras. The theory of relativity shelved the separate notions of space and time and fused them into a single space-time. The interconversion of mass and energy has facilitated atomic studies, allowed the harnessing of nuclear power, and shed light onto the big bang theory for the creation of the world. Though Einstein never succeeded in discovering a grand unifying theory and was even ridiculed for trying to do so, today's physicists have returned to this problem. In 1952, a new element, atomic number 99, was discovered. It was named einsteinium, after the man who changed the way the world looked at matter, time, and space.

CHRONOLOGY

1879	Albert Einstein is born March 14th in Ulm, Germany
1896–1900	Studies at the Swiss Federal Polytechnic Institute in Zurich, Switzerland
1902	Begins working at the Swiss patent office in Bern
1905	Einstein obtains a doctorate degree in physics from the University of Zurich. He also publishes landmark papers describing the nature of light, explaining Brownian motion, and proposing the special theory of relativity
1908	Becomes an unpaid lecturer at the University of Bern
1909	Is appointed associate professor at the University of Zurich and resigns from the patent office
1911	Becomes a full professor at the German University of Prague
1914	Becomes a professor at the University of Berlin and head of the Kaiser Wilhelm Physical Institute
1916	Publishes his general theory of relativity
1919	Sir Arthur Stanley Eddington confirms predictions about the apparent position of certain stars based on Einstein's general theory of relativity, thrusting Einstein into the limelight
1921	Einstein is awarded the Nobel Prize in physics for his services to theoretical physics and especially for his discovery of the law of the photoelectric effect
1929	Publishes his first version of unified field theory
1933	Leaves Germany to accept a position at the Institute for Advanced Study in Princeton, New Jersey
1939	Writes President Franklin D. Roosevelt, supporting the development of an atomic bomb
1952	Is offered the presidency of Israel but declines
1955	Dies April 18th in Princeton, New Jersey, at the age of 76, from a ruptured aorta

FURTHER READING

Bodanis, David. $E = mc^2$: *A Biography of the World's Most Famous Equation*. New York: Walker and Company, 2000. An in-depth explanation of the equation and the scientific history leading to its formulation.

"Einstein Revealed." Nova Online, WGBH Educational Foundation. Available online. URL: http://www.pbs.org/wgbh/nova/einstein. Accessed on January 30, 2005. This site is based on a NOVA program originally aired in 1996 and contains links to a time line, games to help students understand Einstein's science, the impact of his discoveries, and more.

Garraty, John A., and Mark C. Carnes, eds. *American National Biography*. Vol. 8. New York: Oxford University Press, 1999. Brief accounts of the lives and works of famous Americans in encyclopedia format.

Goldsmith, Donald. *The Ultimate Einstein*. New York: Byron Preiss, 1997. Describes Einstein's personal life, his revolutionary theories about time, space, and light, and the ramifications of his work.

Nobelprize.org. "The Nobel Prize in Physics 1921." Available online. URL: http://nobelprize.org/physics/laureates/1921. Last modified on June 16, 2000. Contains links for Einstein's biography, Nobel lecture, and other related resources.

Strathern, Paul. *The Big Idea: Einstein and Relativity*. New York: Anchor Books, 1999. A short, easy-to-read book that helps explain what relativity means and what its implications are.

7

Niels Bohr

(1885–1962)

Niels Bohr proposed a model of atomic structure based on spectroscopy and quantum theory. (© *The Nobel Foundation*)

A Quantum Mechanical Model of the Atom

Just as there are natural laws one must follow when ascending or descending a staircase, there are restrictions to the movements and positions of electrons within an atom. The quantum mechanical model of the atom requires that electrons occupy defined orbits. In the staircase analogy, steps represent defined orbits of an atom, and try as one may, a person cannot hover in between the steps of a staircase. When one orbit is filled, additional electrons cannot join that same orbit, just as only a limited number of people may occupy a single step. This hypothetical staircase has steps of different heights, representing the different amounts of energy required to move from one specific orbit to another, with larger steps requiring more energy to ascend. Orbits nearer to the nucleus are lower in energy, and orbits farther away from the nucleus are higher in energy. Likewise, the higher one ascends a staircase, the more energy it takes. The quantum mechanical model of the atom illustrated by this staircase analogy was proposed by the Danish theoretical physicist Niels Bohr, earning him the Nobel Prize in physics for 1929.

An Impressive Scientific Pedigree

Niels Henrik David Bohr was born on October 7, 1885, in Copenhagen, Denmark. His father, Christian Bohr, a distinguished professor of physiology at the University of Copenhagen, was twice nominated for a Nobel Prize. His mother, Ellen Adler Bohr, was the daughter of a successful banker who was a member of Parliament. The Bohr family, which included Niels's older sister, Jenny, and younger brother, Harald, lived in luxurious quarters adjoining the university. Both parents encouraged their son's academic and other interests, such as woodworking and repairing broken clocks and other mechanical items. From first grade through high school Niels attended the Gammelholm School, where he excelled in science and mathematics but dreaded composition.

In 1903, Niels enrolled at the University of Copenhagen, where he majored in physics, played on the soccer team, enjoyed reading poetry, and set a record for breaking glass in the chemistry labs. Physics emerged as his main interest, but few specialty classes were offered in the subject, so Niels sought out much of his physics knowledge from scientific journals. During his sophomore year, the Royal Danish Academy of Sciences and Letters in Copenhagen solicited papers discussing the surface tension of liquids. Only two papers were submitted, and both earned a gold medal. Niel's paper describing a precision measurement of the surface tension from vibrations of waterdrops in a jet was published in the *Philosophical Transactions of the Royal Society* in 1909, an impressive accomplishment for work performed by an undergraduate student.

After receiving a bachelor's degree in physics in 1907, he earned a master's degree in physics in 1909 and a doctorate in 1911. His dissertation was a theoretical analysis on the properties of metals using the *electron theory*. As a graduate student, Bohr became convinced that classical physics alone was not sufficient for explaining atomic phenomena. During his studies, he encountered the quantum theory of radiation that was proposed by Max Planck and stated that energy is transmitted in discrete units, or quanta.

After receiving a Ph.D., Bohr went to Cambridge University to study at the Cavendish Laboratory under the direction of Nobel laureate (physics 1906) Sir Joseph John Thomson, the English physicist famous for discovering the electron. After six months, Bohr transferred to Ernest Rutherford's laboratory at the University of Manchester. Rutherford won the Nobel Prize in chemistry in 1908 for explaining radioactivity and, in 1911, he proposed a new atomic model that placed a dense, positively charged nucleus in the center of orbiting electrons. While in Rutherford's lab, Bohr realized that nuclear charge (which is dependent on the number of protons and equal to the atomic number) was a better determinant for placement of elements in the periodic table than was atomic mass. He also devised the radioactive displacement law. Rutherford previously had described two types of radioactive decay: alpha and beta. The displacement law said that during radioactive decay, if an element emits an alpha particle, it moves two places to the left on the periodic table, and if it emits a beta particle, it gains one unit of charge and moves to the right one position. When Bohr shared this revelation with Rutherford, Rutherford was cautious, so Bohr did not publish it. Meanwhile, Bohr started researching the implications of these findings on atomic structure. He was particularly interested in problems that Rutherford's model of the atom did not explain.

Explanation of an Atomic Conundrum

Classical laws of electrodynamics required that moving particles, such as orbiting electrons, radiate energy. If this was true, and all matter is composed of atoms that contain orbiting electrons, then all matter should emit radiation, but this does not occur. Another problem was that if the electrons gave off energy as they orbited around the nucleus, then they should eventually lose all of their energy and spiral progressively toward the nucleus and eventually collide with it, but atoms were much more stable than this model predicted. Bohr wondered how to explain this paradox.

In 1905, Albert Einstein had applied Planck's quantum theory to explain the photoelectric effect, the phenomenon whereby metal atoms emit electrons after being hit by a beam of light, creating an electric current. Physicists were baffled because brighter lights did not cause more energetic electrons to be emitted, as they expected. As a solution, Einstein suggested that metal atoms released electrons only when a quantum of light, called a photon, had sufficient energy. Brighter light would lead to more quanta and therefore the release of more electrons, but they would all have the same energy content. Colors of light with shorter wavelengths (such as blue) were associated with quanta that contained high amounts of energy, thus they would induce the emission of more energetic electrons. Colors with longer wavelengths (such as reds) were associated with quanta containing less energy, maybe not enough to cause the release of any electrons from the metal atoms, no matter how bright. Bohr contemplated this concept that earned Einstein the 1921 Nobel Prize in physics.

Bohr thought perhaps electrons could retain their energy and thus continue to orbit the nucleus if they remained in certain defined orbital pathways. The electrons could jump to higher or lower energy orbits by the respective input or release of specific amounts of energy (quanta). While Bohr was pondering this possibility, he came across a paper that related the unusual corona of the Sun with the quantum theory written by King's College mathematics professor J. W. Nicholson. What was the connection between the emission spectra of an element and its atomic con-

struction? An *emission spectrum* is a specific pattern of lines representing certain wavelengths of radiation emitted by a heated chemical element. The patterns are characteristic for each element, like
fingerprints. The threat of competition to be the first to explain this mystery, as well as the realization that quanta might help solve it, stimulated Bohr to solve this puzzle quickly.

After completing his postdoctoral year of research in Rutherford's laboratory, Bohr returned to Denmark and married Margrethe Nørlund in 1912, a partnership that would last for 50 years. They had six sons during the period 1916–28, including one (Aage) who won the Nobel Prize in physics in 1975 for work on the structure of the atomic nucleus. Bohr desired a professorship at the University of Copenhagen, but only one such position existed, and it was filled. He accepted a lectureship in physics and continued filling in the framework of his new model for atomic structure.

He focused on the hydrogen atom because it contained a single electron. Culmination came when Bohr recognized a mathematical connection

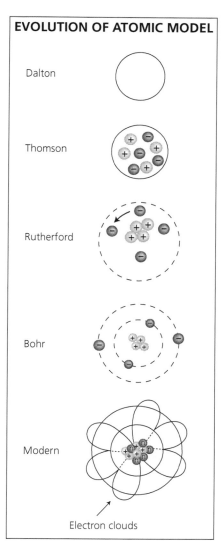

EVOLUTION OF ATOMIC MODEL

Dalton

Thomson

Rutherford

Bohr

Modern

Electron clouds

Once considered the smallest unit of matter, the model of the architecture of an atom has become quite complex.

Quantum Superstars

The German physicist Max Planck gets credit for originally proposing the concept of quanta, the idea that energy is transmitted in discrete allowed quantities. In the 1920s, the concept blossomed into a completely new field of physics called quantum mechanics as several young physicists made a series of breakthroughs. Quantum mechanics attempts to describe the behavior of particles at the atomic level. A few key founders of quantum mechanics are mentioned below.

In 1924, the French physicist Louis de Broglie suggested that all matter exhibited behavior characteristic of both waves and particles but that wave characteristics were only observable at the atomic level. This concept developed into the field of wave mechanics, which grew into quantum mechanics, and earned de Broglie the 1929 Nobel Prize in physics.

In 1925, the Austrian physicist Wolfgang Pauli announced that in any system of elementary particles, no two particles may move in the same way. In other words, no two electrons could occupy the same energy

between the emission of radiation and Planck's constant. The amount of energy necessary for an electron to change energy levels was equal to $h\nu$, with h being Planck's constant and ν being the frequency. He used this relationship to predict the frequencies of radiation emitted for orbital shifts of hydrogen's single electron, and miraculously, they all proved correct! His calculations accounted for the series of lines in the emission spectrum for hydrogen; he had solved the problem of electron motion. Bohr's amended model of an atom included defined stationary orbits with discrete radii for electrons, so they could not spiral toward the nucleus. As long as an

state simultaneously. This came to be known as the Pauli *exclusion principle* and explained why all the electrons of an atom did not occupy the lowest energy level. Pauli won the Nobel Prize in physics in 1945.

The Austrian physicist Erwin Schrödinger formulated a useful equation in 1926 that described how electrons behave in an atom and is now considered the origin of quantum mechanics. The English physicist Paul Adrien Maurice Dirac extended Schrödinger's work to more fully describe an electron's properties, allowing the prediction of an electron's *spin* and magnetic charge. Dirac and Schrödinger shared the Nobel Prize in physics in 1933.

In 1926, the German physicist Max Born said that the rise and fall of waves represented the fluctuating probability that an electron behaved like a particle. For this he shared the 1954 Nobel Prize in physics with the German physicist Walther Wilhelm Georg Franz Bothe.

The Heisenberg *uncertainty principle,* proposed by the German physicist Werner Karl Heisenberg in 1927, stated that the position and the velocity of an electron cannot be determined accurately at the same time. One only could predict statistically where an electron will go when it is hit. Unable to reconcile with the idea of not being able to know something, Albert Einstein never accepted this principle that earned Heisenberg the 1932 Nobel Prize in physics.

electron remained within an orbit, it did not radiate energy. If an electron fell to a lower energy level, the atom would radiate a quantum of light equal to the specific amount of energy lost by the electron during the transition, accounting for the specific patterns of wavelengths in the emission spectra of specific elements.

As he wrote up his radical discovery, Bohr realized it was too much to fit into one scientific paper, so he split the content into a trilogy of articles that were all published in *Philosophical Magazine* in 1913. These revolutionary papers were titled "On the Constitution of Atoms and Molecules," "Systems Containing Only a Single Nucleus," and "Systems Containing Several Nuclei." What Bohr proposed was so extraordinary that some scientists reportedly promised to give up physics if his ideas turned out to be true. They were true and, in 1922, Bohr received the Nobel Prize in physics for developing this quantum mechanical model of the atom.

The man who two years prior could only obtain a lectureship became highly recruited as acceptance of his ideas spread. Bohr accepted a two-year readership at the University of Manchester in 1913. Though the University of Copenhagen had just offered him a professorship in theoretical physics, the first such professorship, Bohr could not resist the opportunity to work alongside Rutherford once more. Copenhagen delayed his start date until 1916 to accommodate Bohr's wishes.

Correspondence and Complementarity

Quantum theory satisfied some enigmatic phenomena, but sometimes its approach appeared to conflict with classical laws. To bridge the gap between classical and quantum theories, in 1916, Bohr proposed the principle of *correspondence*, which stated that any conclusion drawn from quantum physics must not conflict with any observable phenomena. Theoretical studies must agree with or correspond to the real world as described by the older classical physical theories.

As papers related to the developing infant field of quantum mechanics flooded the journals, Bohr began raising money to found an institute devoted to theoretical physics. The inauguration of the Institute for Theoretical Physics in Copenhagen occurred in September 1921, and the center quickly became a hub of intellectual activity. As the director, 36-year-old Bohr recruited and encouraged the brightest minds, and throughout the 1920s and 1930s, the young scientists continuously produced breakthroughs in the changing field of physics. Bohr continued to extend his atomic theory to higher elements and summarized his work in "The Structure of the Atoms and the Physical and Chemical Properties of the Elements" in 1922. He also developed another new fundamental concept.

In 1927, Bohr introduced the concept of *complementarity*, stating that a classical description of an atomic phenomenon requires knowledge of two complementary phenomena, such as *momentum* and position of an electron. The two complementary aspects could not be observed simultaneously—they are mutually exclusive, but both are valid and indispensable, and together they represent a more complete description of small-scale phenomena. This attempt to reconcile classical physics with the new quantum physics could be applied to light, for example, which could behave as a particle and as a wave but not both at the same time. The Copenhagen Interpretation of quantum mechanics, named so because Bohr was a main proponent, and he lived in Copenhagen, was an attempt to explain what happens in the quantum world, taking into account the principles of complementarity and uncertainty. Since attempts to measure the quantum world necessarily disturb it, Bohr claimed it was pointless to ask what quantum entities were doing when they were not being observed. Max Born said one could only calculate the probability of achieving a particular result.

Bohr extended his principle of complementarity from science to other aspects of life. He outlined his philosophy on these matters in multiple essays published between 1933–62.

Looking Inward

In 1932, Bohr became a permanent resident of the Residence of Honor on the Carlsberg brewery grounds, an honor bestowed only to the most prominent of Danish citizens. Around this time, he began focusing on the center of the atom, the nucleus, which scientists by then knew contained both protons and neutrons. He thought physicists should depart from the notion that atomic nuclei were rigid bodies. In 1936, he developed an idea originally proposed by the Ukrainian astrophysicist George Gamow suggesting the atomic nucleus resembled a liquid droplet. Just as the shape of a droplet of liquid changes as the assemblage forces between its molecules change, the shape of an atomic nucleus changes in response to dynamic interactions between its protons and neutrons. This theory helped explain the process of nuclear fission that was interpreted in 1939 by Lise Meitner and Otto Frisch. The liquid droplet theory allows for the formation of a highly excited compound nucleus when impinging particles bombard an atomic nucleus. Then the nucleus either disintegrates into the original unaltered particles, into the same particles but with altered energies, or forms new particles during a nuclear reaction. During nuclear fission, a nucleus splits into two parts (two smaller droplets), and energy is released.

The 1930s were filled with personal tragedy for Bohr, who suffered the loss of his mother, sister, son, and two close colleagues, Rutherford and Paul Ehrenfest. In addition, World War II broke out. Bohr was instrumental in assisting the escape and placement of many scientists threatened by the Nazi regime into positions outside of Germany. In October 1943, Bohr fled to Sweden to escape arrest by the Nazis. The rest of his family followed and then proceeded to England and the United States, where he consulted for the top secret Manhattan Project to build the first atomic bomb. Bohr was as concerned about the political implications nuclear weapons would have on the world as he was about the physical mechanics of their development. He made repeated attempts to keep atomic weapons under civilian rather than military control and to convince world leaders that cooperation with the Russians was the best means to forestall competition in the nuclear arms race, but his dream of mutual trust and international cooperation in the development of nuclear weapons was not realized during his lifetime.

Bohr's Legacy

In his later years, Bohr visited the Institute for Advanced Study at Princeton, New Jersey, where Einstein worked. Though Einstein and Bohr debated fiercely for decades about quantum mechanics, Bohr greatly respected and admired Einstein. Bohr helped organize the European Council for Nuclear Research (CERN), an international center for theoretical and experimental physics, and the

Nordic Institute for Theoretical Physics (NORDITA), a theoretical physics consortium for Norway, Sweden, Finland, Denmark, and Iceland. In 1957, he accepted the first Ford Foundation Atoms for Peace Award for his efforts to develop peaceful uses of atomic energy.

A minor cerebral hemorrhage in 1962 slowed Bohr down, but he seemed to recover and went back to work a few months later. He chaired a meeting of the Danish Royal Academy of Sciences on November 16, 1962. Two days later, he died of heart failure in Copenhagen. The whole world mourned the passing of this great man who loved talking and sports as much as he did science.

Despite his administrative duties, Bohr never stopped doing scientific research and published over 200 scientific articles. On what would have been Bohr's 80th birthday, the Institute for Theoretical Physics at the University of Copenhagen was renamed the Niels Bohr Institute. During Bohr's tenure as director, over 1,200 articles were published from Copenhagen and the institute was a world-class center for theoretical physics. Bohr was awarded almost three-dozen honorary doctorate degrees from universities all over the world, including Cambridge, Oxford, Manchester, Harvard, Princeton, and Edinburgh, and he received numerous prestigious awards, including the Max Planck Medal of the German Physical Society (1930), the Hughes (1921) and the Copley (1938) Medals from the Royal Society of London, and the Faraday Medal of the Chemical Society of London (1930). He served as president of the Royal Danish Academy of Sciences (1939–62) and as chairman of the Danish Atomic Energy Commission. He was a foreign member of at least 22 academic organizations, including the Royal Society of London.

Bohr's quantum mechanical model of the atom with electrons in defined orbits is familiar to most students of physics, chemistry, and biology, but his legacy extends beyond his intellectual contributions. Bohr was a role model and an encourager to many future Nobel recipients, and his leadership helped usher in the age of quantum mechanics. Because of this, he is considered one of the most distinguished Danish citizens of all time, and indeed, one of the world's greatest pioneering physicists.

CHRONOLOGY

1885	Niels Bohr is born October 7th in Copenhagen, Denmark
1905	Performs research on the surface tension of water
1907	Receives a bachelor's degree in physics from the University of Copenhagen
1909	Earns a master's degree in physics from the University of Copenhagen
1911	Receives a doctorate degree in physics from the University of Copenhagen and travels to Cambridge to study at the Cavendish Laboratory, headed by Sir Joseph John Thomson
1912	Completes postdoctoral research at the University of Manchester with Ernest Rutherford
1913	Publishes trilogy of articles in *Philosophical Magazine* describing his quantum mechanical model of the atom
1913–14	Lectures in physics at the University of Copenhagen
1914–16	Holds a readership position at the University of Manchester
1916	Becomes first professor of theoretical physics at the University of Copenhagen and proposes principle of correspondence
1921	Becomes the first director of the new Institute for Theoretical Physics in Copenhagen. He retains this position until his death
1922	Receives Nobel Prize in physics for his theory of the quantum mechanical model of the atom
1927	Introduces principle of complementarity
1936	Develops liquid droplet theory to describe the atomic nucleus
1943–45	Consults for the Manhattan Project
1955	Retires from teaching but continues to serve as director of the Institute for Theoretical Physics

| 1962 | Dies November 18th of heart failure at age 77, in Copenhagen |

FURTHER READING

Bohr, Niels. *Atomic Theory and the Description of Nature.* London: Cambridge University Press, 1961. Reprints of four original Bohr articles, with a helpful introductory survey.

Nobelprize.org. "The Nobel Prize in Physics 1922." Available online. URL: http://nobelprize.org/physics/ laureates/ 1922. Last modified on June 16, 2000. Contains links for Bohr's biography, Nobel lecture, and other related resources.

Pasachoff, Naomi. *Niels Bohr: Physicist and Humanitarian.* Berkeley Heights, N.J.: Enslow, 2003. Biography written for juvenile readers that discusses Bohr's contributions to the development of quantum theory and cooperation among scientists.

Scientists and Inventors. New York: Macmillan Library Reference, 1998. Brief profiles of the lives and works of more than 100 notable scientists, written for juvenile readers.

Spangenburg, Ray, and Diane K. Moser. *Niels Bohr: Gentle Genius of Denmark.* New York: Facts On File, 1995. Part of the Makers of Modern Science set written for young adults, describes the effect of Bohr's intellectual contributions on the progress of science.

Louis de Broglie

(1892–1987)

Louis de Broglie introduced the wave matter composition of electrons to quantum theory. (© *The Nobel Foundation*)

The Foundation of Wave Mechanics

The fact that something cannot easily be observed does not mean it does not happen. Humans do not have the ability to perceive certain processes, though they might occur openly. For example, one might mow the lawn one afternoon, only to find a dandelion towering inches above the cut grass the following day. Even if someone watched the weed for 24 hours straight, he could not see it grow, that is, he could not determine the amount of growth that appeared by continuously watching it with just his eyes. If a camera shot a picture of the stem every 30 minutes and then one viewed the frames in rapid succession, the growth would appear continuous even though the frames would be jumping. Things are not always what they seem. On the other hand, though a bowling ball rolling down an aisle is an easily observable motion that can be described using classical laws of physics, the ball is not simply just matter, something that has mass and occupies space, but it also is a wave motion and can be described differently in terms of properties typically associated with waves. The wavelength is so small relative to the size of the ball, however, that it is imperceptible. An electron, also considered a particle of matter, also may be described in terms of its wave characteristics. Its waves can be detected experimentally, since the associated wavelength is larger with respect to the size of the electron. A theoretical physicist named Louis de Broglie came up with the concept that matter is dual-natured, both particulate and wavelike. His mathematical proof of this idea entirely changed the way scientists think about matter.

An Aristocratic Family

Louis-Victor-Pierre-Raymond de Broglie was born to Victor de Broglie and Pauline d'Armaillé de Broglie on August 15, 1892, in Dieppe, France. His father, who held the inherited title of duke, died when Louis was 14 years old, and the eldest son, Maurice, became a duke, a title held only by the male head of the family. All the family members shared the title prince, bestowed upon the de Broglies by the Austrians after the Seven Years' War (1756–63). After his brother's death in 1906, Louis was both a prince and a duke. The youngest of five siblings, Louis received his primary education at home and his secondary education at the Lyceé Janson de Sailly in Paris, graduating in 1909. At the Sorbonne, the arts faculty of the University of Paris, Louis studied literature and history, with plans to embark on a civil service career, but he became interested in mathematics and physics. After obtaining a bachelor of arts degree from the Sorbonne in 1910, he decided to pursue a degree in theoretical physics.

After receiving his Licencié ès Sciences from the University of Paris's Faculté des Sciences in 1913, de Broglie served in the French army during World War I, at which time he learned about wireless telegraphy and served as a radio specialist. After the war, he continued his studies of physics in his brother's private laboratory. Several breakthroughs and new developments in the quantum theory that was proposed by Max Planck in 1900 revolutionized physics in the 1920s. De Broglie's doctoral dissertation, "Recherches sur la théorie des quanta" (Research on the quantum theory), published in the *Annales de Physique* in 1925, concluded that matter has both properties of waves and particles and was an important impetus for this revolution.

The Problem

Throughout the 19th century, physicists gathered data supporting the wavelike nature of light. Then Albert Einstein came along in 1905 and proposed a new theory of light. By applying Planck's concept of quanta to radiation, Einstein concluded that light is transmitted in tiny particles of specific energy, now called photons, rather than as waves. Einstein's theoretically deduced equations were experimentally verified by American physicist Robert Andrews Millikan in 1913 and 1914. American physicist Arthur Holly Compton provided further support for the photon theory of light in 1923 when he explained the X-ray scattering phenomenon called the Compton effect. When a photon hit an electron, the photon lost energy, resulting in a larger wavelength (shorter wavelengths are associated with higher energy); thus, Compton showed that photons have momentum, a property of particles. Despite the new experimentally sound evidence for light being particulate in nature, light clearly also possessed well-documented, wavelike qualities, and physicists hesitantly began to accept the fact that light was of a dual nature, sometimes exhibiting wavelike properties and sometimes particulate properties.

This revelation shattered the previously accepted partitioned view of the physical world that consisted of two realms—matter and energy. Because all matter is composed of atoms, the physics of

What Is a Wave?

A wave is a traveling disturbance that moves energy from one place to another without moving matter. Waves are created by oscillations in a medium and propagate away from the source. Waves can be classified into two main types: transverse or longitudinal. Transverse waves vibrate at right angles to the direction of movement. For example, when one wriggles a rope up and down, the wave propagates horizontally, but the vibrations are vertical. Longitudinal waves move in the same direction as the oscillations and are characterized by areas of compression and rarefaction (expansion). Sound waves are an example of this type.

Waves are characterized by three properties: wavelength, frequency, and *amplitude*. The wavelength is the distance from the point on one wave to a point in the identical position on the adjacent wave. The frequency equals the number of vibrations per second and has the unit Hertz. The amplitude is the highest point reached above the average height by a wave. The speed or velocity of a wave is the product of the wavelength and the frequency.

Reflection and *refraction* are typical wavelike behaviors. A wave is reflected when it hits an obstacle and at least part of it bounces back. For example, an echo is the reflection of sound waves. Refraction occurs

matter was concerned with atoms and corpuscles that obeyed the classical laws of physics. Radiation, the manifestation of pure energy, on the other hand, was based on the propagation of waves through a hypothetical medium. The form of matter and the form of radiation had been considered to be structured differently until linked through the discovery that light, or radiant energy, was dual-natured.

when a wave hits a boundary for a different medium and the wave's direction is altered. This is apparent when you view an object held underwater and it appears blurry. When two waves pass through the same space at the same time, *interference* occurs. The interference is considered constructive if their *crests* (highest points) arrive at the same place at the same time. Destructive interference occurs when the crest of one wave and the *trough* (lowest point) of another wave arrive at the same place at the same time, canceling each other out. Oftentimes, interference is only partially destructive. *Diffraction* is the phenomenon whereby waves must bend around an obstacle to move past it.

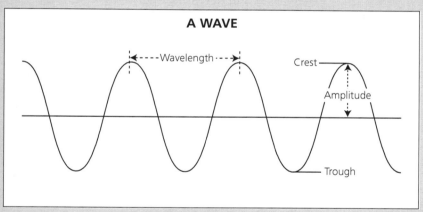

A WAVE

Wavelength and amplitude are two defining characteristics of a wave.

De Broglie went one step further. He wondered, if light was dual-natured, then what about matter? Though observably particulate in nature, might matter also have wavelike characteristics? Symmetry of nature suggested that corpuscles would be associated with waves. This is the topic de Broglie chose for his doctoral thesis, a thesis that was worthy of the 1929 Nobel Prize in physics.

Revolutionary Thesis

Without any supporting facts, the bold graduate student de Broglie purported that "matter waves" were associated with everything; though not apparent at a macroscopic level, wavelike behavior could be detected at the atomic level. All objects have matter waves, but they are so small compared to the object itself that they are virtually imperceptible. At the atomic level, their size is relatively large in comparison, and they are detectable. De Broglie said that possession of both wavelike and particle-like properties was not simultaneously impossible but required different perspectives. The seemingly conflicting characteristics were not mutually exclusive; however, one could not perceive both aspects at the same time, just as one cannot directly view the back of someone's head and their face at the same time. He backed up his complicated proposition with mathematical analysis using Einstein's generalized equations of relativity that already defined a relationship between energy, matter, and Planck's constant. De Broglie assigned a frequency and a wavelength to particles and found that $\lambda = h/p$ (with p representing momentum, a property of matter equal to the product of mass and velocity). He mathematically demonstrated that particles had matter waves.

De Broglie's wave theory explained why electrons can only exist in discrete orbits, as proposed by Niels Bohr. According to de Broglie, the orbits were not smooth, circular paths but wavy paths wrapped around the nucleus of the atom. A whole number of waves was required to complete the orbit to avoid any interference. So orbits were dependent on electron wavelengths, which de Broglie discovered to be dependent on momentum, which Bohr had predicted must be an exact multiple of Planck's constant.

The faculty members on de Broglie's dissertation committee did not feel intellectually qualified to evaluate the profound thesis, so they recommended that Einstein read it. Scientists today still have difficulty comprehending the content and significance of de Broglie's proclamations. Einstein was very capable, however, and his declaration that de Broglie had discovered one of the secrets of the universe forced others to consider the dual nature of matter. De Broglie's hypothesis made Einstein's contention that energy and mass were interconvertible more understandable. The Austrian physicist Erwin Schrödinger also grasped the significance of the wave concept and used it to develop a wave equation to describe the behavior of an electron in an atom, earning him the Nobel Prize in physics in 1933.

Proof and Debate

When de Broglie proposed the matter-wave relation, he had no supporting facts, but the proof for the wave nature of electrons did follow. In 1927, Clinton Joseph Davisson and Lester Halbert Germer at the Bell laboratories in New York serendipitously discovered that crystals diffracted an electron beam, and diffraction was a property of waves. The mathematical calculations from their experiments agreed with de Broglie's formula. Later that same year, the English physicist Sir George Paget Thomson (son of the famous Cambridge physicist Sir Joseph John Thomson) observed diffraction by passing electrons through metallic foil. Davisson and Thomson shared the 1937 Nobel Prize in physics for their experimental discovery of the diffraction of electrons. Experimental evidence later produced similar results for protons, atoms, and molecules.

After receiving a doctorate from the Sorbonne, de Broglie taught there for two years. He attended the 1927 seventh Solvay conference, where the most prominent physicists of the time debated wave mechanics and its implications. Some, such as the German physicist Werner Karl Heisenberg, the Danish physicist Niels Bohr, and the English physicist Max Born, believed that the rise and fall of waves simply represented the probability of the position of a particle rather than its exact position. Others, such as Schrödinger, Einstein, and de Broglie disagreed. De Broglie proposed what he called the pilot wave theory in response, but this theory was flawed. Aware of this, he temporarily abandoned it, but returned to it decades later, seeking an alternative to the probabilistic interpretation. Philosophically, de Broglie could not accept that the world acted in a random manner.

Founder of a New Field

In 1928 de Broglie became a professor of theoretical physics at the Henri Poincaré Institute and in 1932, a professor of theoretical physics at the Faculté des Sciences at the Sorbonne, where he remained until his retirement in 1962. At the Sorbonne he extended his research on wave mechanics. He authored dozens of books related to wave mechanics and the philosophical implications of the quantum physics, including *Matter and Light: The New Physics* in 1939 and *The Revolution in Physics* in 1953. Though these are less technical than many of his works, they are still quite complicated due to the nature of their content.

He was elected to the Académie des Sciences in 1933 and served as permanent secretary for the mathematical sciences from 1942 until his death. The academy awarded de Broglie their Poincaré Medal in 1929 and the Albert I of Monaco Prize in 1932. In 1943, he established a center for applied mechanics at the Henri Poincaré Institute. The United Nations Educational, Scientific, and Cultural Organization (UNESCO) awarded de Broglie the Kalinga Prize in 1952 for his efforts to popularize physics and make it understandable for the general public. The French National Center for Scientific Research presented him with a gold medal in 1955. He also was bestowed with many honorary degrees and belonged to several international academic organizations, including the National Academy of Sciences of the United States and the Royal Society of London. Prince Louis de Broglie died at age 94, on March 19, 1987, in Paris, France.

De Broglie interpreted physical phenomena in an entirely new manner and in doing so, helped physicists better understand the behavior of matter, especially at the atomic level. His proposal that every moving particle is associated with waves helped to fuse the concepts of particles and waves, cementing the duality of nature and laying a foundation for modern theoretical physics. As a proponent of one of the most significant advances in the field, he is appropriately titled the founder of wave mechanics.

CHRONOLOGY

1892	Louis-Victor-Pierre-Raymond de Broglie is born August 15th at Dieppe, France
1909	Graduates from the Lyceé Janson de Sailly in Paris
1910	Receives a bachelor of arts degree from the Sorbonne at the University of Paris
1913	Obtains Licencié ès Sciences from the University of Paris's Faculté des Sciences
1924	Completes doctoral thesis "Recherches sur la théorie des quanta" (Research on the quantum theory)
1928	Becomes professor of theoretical physics at the Henri Poincaré Institute
1929	Receives Nobel Prize in physics for his discovery of the wave nature of electrons
1932	Becomes professor of theoretical physics at the Faculté des Sciences at the Sorbonne
1945	Becomes technical adviser to the French Atomic Energy Commission
1962	Retires from the Sorbonne
1987	Dies of natural causes March 19th in Paris, France

FURTHER READING

Boorse, Henry A., Lloyd Motz, and Jefferson Hane Weaver. *The Atomic Scientists: A Biographical History.* New York: John Wiley,

1989. Chronological presentation of physicists who made significant contributions to understanding the atom.

Encyclopedia of World Biography. 2nd Edition, Vol. 3. Detroit, Mich.: Gale Research, 1998. Brief biographies of notable figures and summaries of their accomplishments written for high school students.

Magill, Frank N., ed. *Dictionary of World Biography*. Vol. 7. *The 20th Century*. Pasadena, Calif.: Salem Press, 1999. Chronological arrangements of important world figures written for young adults.

Nobelprize.org. "The Nobel Prize in Physics 1929." Available online. URL: http://nobelprize.org/physics/laureates/1929. Last modified on June 16, 2000. Contains links for de Broglie's biography, Nobel lecture, and other related resources.

Olson, Richard, ed. *Biographical Encyclopedia of Scientists*. Vol. 1. New York: Marshall Cavendish, 1998. Clear, concise summary of major events in the scientists' lives at an accessible level.

9

Richard Feynman

(1918–1988)

Richard Feynman won a Nobel Prize for his reformulation of the theory of quantum electrodynamics. (© The Nobel Foundation)

Development of the Theory of Quantum Electrodynamics

Those who knew him have described the eccentric Nobel laureate Dick Feynman as the "finest physicist of his generation" and the "best-loved scientist of modern times." No ordinary genius, Feynman performed pioneering work on *quantum electrodynamics* (QED), the theory that illustrates the behavior of electrically charged particles, such as electrons, and their interaction with electromagnetic radiation. Not only did he reformulate QED, which has been called the most perfect theory of physics, but he also made it more accessible by simplifying the complex calculations using a graphical method of tracking particles and their interactions. Physicists still use Feynman's diagrams to represent physical processes and the mathematical expressions that describe them.

Early Signs of Genius

Richard Phillips Feynman was born on May 11, 1918, to Melville and Lucille Phillips Feynman (pronounced FINE-man) in New York, New York. Melville, the son of Lithuanian Jews and a sales manager for a uniform business, taught his son, Ritty, to explore nature, ask questions, and seek understanding rather than memorize facts. When he was nine, his mother gave birth to a daughter, Joan, who later earned a Ph.D. in solid-state physics and became a space scientist at the Jet Propulsion Laboratory in Pasadena, California. Ritty once asked his father why a ball in a wagon appeared to roll backward when he pulled the wagon forward, and why the stopped ball rolled forward when he stopped pulling the wagon. His father admitted that nobody knew the answer to that question; scientists called the phenomenon inertia, but nobody could explain why it was true. This early lesson about the nature of physics stuck with Ritty even as he developed into one of the world's most famous physicists.

For many years, the Feynmans shared a house in Far Rockaway, New York, with Lucille's sister's family. Ritty showed early intellectual promise, learning algebra from eavesdropping on his older cousin's tutoring sessions and teaching himself Euclidean geometry. The basement served as a makeshift chemistry laboratory, and a local teacher repaid the prepubescent prodigy's assistance in cleaning up the high school chemistry laboratory by teaching him about atoms. By the time Ritty reached high school, the regular math curriculum bored him, so he taught himself calculus. A very brief struggle in solid geometry gave him an appreciation for the frustrations ordinary people face when learning difficult concepts. Another incident from his formative years that made a lasting impression on Ritty was a conversation with his physics teacher about the principle of least action. Feynman later recalled his excitement at the ability to describe nature by the expression of simple laws that represented deep truths.

Feynman received top honors in almost everything when he graduated from high school in Far Rockaway in 1935, but Columbia University rejected his application because it had already filled its quota of Jewish students. After spending a summer performing odd jobs at his aunt's hotel, he moved to Cambridge, where he enrolled at the Massachusetts Institute of Technology (MIT). As an undergraduate, he joined a fraternity, struggled to pass his humanities courses, and aced graduate-level physics classes. The faculty recognized their student, now called Dick, to be especially gifted in physics and tried to convince the MIT authorities to allow him to graduate after only three years, but their attempt failed. In 1939, Feynman coauthored (with faculty member M. S. Vallarta) a letter to the editor of *Physical Review* (1939) titled "Scattering of Cosmic Rays by the Stars of a Galaxy," in which he calculated the behavior of *cosmic rays* that originated from outside the Milky Way. To fulfill his degree requirement of performing original research, Dick studied the electrostatic forces in crystals, and a condensed version of his senior thesis, "Forces in Molecules" appeared in *Physical Review* later that year.

Princeton and the War

When Feynman entered MIT, he had planned to study mathematics but quickly switched to electrical engineering and then to physics, a field that had recently undergone a major revolution. Since 1900, when the German physicist Max Planck proposed that energy existed in packets called quanta, physicists had been establishing the foundation of quantum mechanics, the branch of physics dealing with the structure and behavior of matter. Whereas classical theories proved useful in describing the behavior of many objects, they failed to explain newer observations of atoms and subatomic particles. During the 1920s, major advances included the discovery of quantized electron orbitals of atoms, the notion of

Paul Dirac

English physicist Paul Adrien Maurice Dirac (August 8, 1902–October 20, 1984), the Lucasian Professor of Mathematics at Cambridge University, was one of the leaders in the quantum revolution in physics during the 1920s. Along with the Austrian theoretical physicist Wolfgang Pauli (1900–58) and the German physicist Werner Karl Heisenberg (1901–76), Dirac was a major contributor in the formulation of the key principles of quantum electrodynamics (QED), the study of the interaction between atomic particles, such as electrons, and electromagnetic radiation. In 1928, he proposed a modified, fuller version of the Schrödinger wave equation that mathematically described the behavior of an electron in an atom. Beginning with information on an electron's mass and charge, he developed equations that predicted additional characteristics such as spin and magnetic charge. Dirac's equation also predicted the existence of a positively charged electron, a *positron*, for

wave-particle duality of light and matter, and the uncertainty principle, stating that is was impossible to know both the momentum and location of a particle at one time. Feynman was spellbound by quantum mechanics and irresistibly drawn in by its seemingly complex questions.

Though he wanted to stay at MIT, Feynman's teachers urged him to complete his education elsewhere. The scores from his standardized tests puzzled the graduate admissions committee at Princeton University; literature, history, and fine arts were weak in contrast to mathematics and physics, which were almost perfect. Recommendations from the MIT faculty persuaded them that

which the American physicist Carl David Anderson detected evidence in 1932. Dirac shared the 1933 Nobel Prize in physics with the Austrian physicist Erwin Schrödinger for their work on the wave equation.

Though Dirac's QED theory was a major advancement in helping scientists to predict the effects of charged particles on each other, it contained flaws; most significantly, the calculations imposed infinite masses and electric charges onto electrons. In addition, the American physicist Willis Lamb (1913–   ) observed behavior involving a tiny difference in energy levels between two electron orbitals in the hydrogen atom that violated predictions from Dirac's equation, a discovery known as the Lamb shift.

Dirac wrote the first physics text explaining quantum mechanics, *The Principles of Quantum Mechanics* (1930), now considered a classic in the field. The second edition, published the same year that Feynman began college (1935), formally introduced Feynman to QED. Reading Dirac's text led him to the conclusion that the existing quantum theory of electricity and magnetism was flawed. The book's closing sentence particularly impressed him, "It seems that some essentially new physical ideas are here needed."

Feynman was an up-and-coming star in physics, and he moved to New Jersey after receiving a bachelor's degree in physics in 1939. Common interests and compatible personalities led Feynman to select as his thesis adviser the young and audacious Professor John Wheeler, with whom he had many discussions on problems plaguing the attempts to quantize electrodynamics.

The timing was such that other unfortunate circumstances demanded Feynman's time during the early 1940s. The United States' involvement in World War II was increasing, and worries about Germany building an atomic bomb prompted American scientists to attempt the same. The majority of the work for the top secret Manhattan Project was being carried out in Los Alamos, New Mexico, but researchers all over the country assisted using resources available at their own universities. Feynman became involved by joining the team of Robert Wilson, a Princeton physicist, whose task was developing a technique for separating radioactive uranium-235 from the more common, stable uranium-238. Feynman also worked on a gauge for measuring explosive pressure.

Feynman had become engaged during his freshman year at MIT to Arline Greenbaum, whom he had dated since high school. In 1941, she became very ill with lymphatic tuberculosis. After learning her diagnosis was fatal, the two decided to marry as soon as Feynman completed his schooling. He already had completed his original research, but he still had to write his dissertation and orally defend it to receive a Ph.D. As her health worsened, Feynman temporarily set aside his war research to write up and defend his dissertation, titled "The Principle of Least Action in Quantum Mechanics." He earned a doctoral degree in theoretical physics in June 1942 and married Arline a few days later.

The head of the Manhattan Project, Julius Robert Oppenheimer, recruited Feynman to Los Alamos in 1943 and was so impressed with his ingenuity that he put him in charge of calculations for the theoretical division the following year. One of his responsibilities was determining the amount of radioactivity that could be stored safely in one place. On June 16, 1945, Arline died. One month later, Feynman witnessed the first atomic bomb explosion with all of the other scientists responsible. He later admitted that though he was confident in his theoretical calculations, seeing the successful final result brought him great relief.

The Most Perfect Theory of Physics

After the war, Cornell University hired Feynman as an associate professor of physics, and he delved back into electrodynamics with renewed energy. Since his undergraduate years, Feynman had wanted to develop a quantum theory that would explain the properties of all matter. Over hundreds of years, scientists had revealed many of nature's secrets by exposing the laws of motion, laws of gravity, and laws of electricity and magnetism. These classical laws explained almost all natural phenomena until the early 20th century, when physicists elucidated the structure of the atom. Physicists then developed the theory of quantum mechanics to explain many observable phenomena at the atomic level and below, but Feynman had never been satisfied with the previous attempts to explain the interaction of light and matter.

As a starting point for his doctoral research, Feynman had considered the problem of infinite self-energy of an electron predicted by existing theory. Field theory described particle interactions in terms of a force field that surrounded charged particles, the strength of which was inversely proportional to the square of the distance between the two particles involved. The problem was that classical field theory required a particle to act on itself, but at zero distance, the strength would be the inverse of zero, imposing infinite self-energy on electrons, and since energy is convertible to mass, infinite mass as well. Feynman concluded that electrons did not act on themselves and went further to reject classical field theory for a modified adjunct theory. In 1945, Wheeler and Feynman published a paper, "Interaction with the Absorber as the Mechanism of Radiation," in *Reviews of Modern Physics*, proposing that half of the electromagnetic field propagated before the electron emitting it accelerated (advanced) and the other half as the electron accelerated (retarded). Several years later, in 1949, they built upon this idea in "Classical Electrodynamics in Terms of Direct Interparticle Action," (*Reviews of Modern Physics*, 1949), showing that classical electrodynamics could be described without the notion of a field, eliminating self-interaction and focusing on how the motion of one charge affects the motion of the other.

After taking care to describe a consistent theory for electrodynamics that addressed the problem of infinite self-energy for an electron, Feynman set out to quantize it, but his peers did not readily accept his unconventional approach. Feynman showed how his procedure explained the Lamb shift of energy levels for hydrogen. He introduced a spacetime view, came up with an improved technique to perform calculations termed the *path integral approach* that led to greater accuracy in predicting subatomic actions and introduced the now famous Feynman diagrams. His reformulation of QED was such an important improvement; whereas Dirac's theory maintained a value of one for the magnetic moment of an electron, Feynman's carried out the predicted value to 1.00115965246 ± 20, in close agreement with the experimentally measured value of 1.00115965221 ± 4.

Arrows and Amplitudes

The best way to explain Feynman's approach to QED is by following through an example that he used to explain the partial reflection of light by glass in his 1985 book, QED: The Strange Theory of Light and Matter. Light is a form of electromagnetic radiation that comes in particles called photons. When light shines on some surfaces, like glass, photons are both reflected and transmitted. When one looks through a window, he or she may see through to the other side in addition to a partial reflection on it. For an individual photon, one cannot predict its behavior, but given many photons, one can measure experimentally the average number of photons and, from that, know the probability that an individual photon will be transmitted or reflected by a single surface of glass—96 percent pass through and 4 percent are reflected. Interestingly, the partial reflection of light by two surfaces (the front and the back of the glass) is not 8 percent, as it would seem (4% + 4% = 8%), but cycles between 0 and 16 percent, depending on the thickness of the glass. If light consisted only of electromagnetic waves, this would make sense, but how can this be explained considering the particulate nature of light, as implied by the concept of quanta of light energy, the photons?

Feynman used arrows, also called amplitudes, to represent the motion of particles. Two arrows represented the reflection from the front surface and from the back surface. The length of an arrow was related to the probability of that event occurring. As a side of a square whose area equaled the probability of an event, the arrow's length equaled the square root of the probability. If an old-fashioned stopwatch (not digital) with a single hand was started when a light source emitted a photon and stopped when the photon reached its destination, a photomultiplier detector, the direction of the stopwatch hand corresponded to the direction of the arrow. For the front surface of the glass, the direction was reversed 180 degrees, and for the back reflection, the direction was the same as the stopwatch hand.

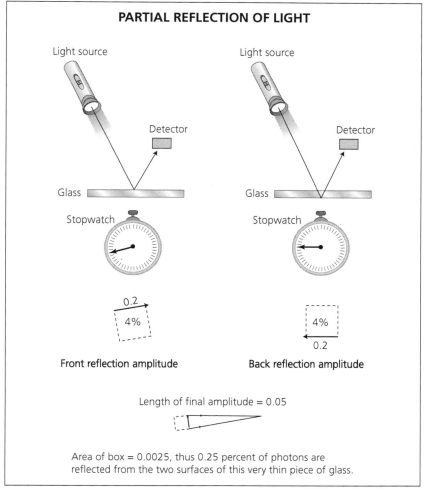

PARTIAL REFLECTION OF LIGHT

Light source

Light source

Detector

Detector

Glass

Glass

Stopwatch

Stopwatch

0.2

4%

4%

0.2

Front reflection amplitude

Back reflection amplitude

Length of final amplitude = 0.05

Area of box = 0.0025, thus 0.25 percent of photons are reflected from the two surfaces of this very thin piece of glass.

The final arrow that represents the probability or amplitude of light being reflected from both surfaces of an extremely thin piece of glass is very short.

The amount of light reflected back from an extremely thin piece of glass is almost zero. This amount can be calculated using Feynman's system of arrows. The length of one arrow represents the probability that light will be reflected from the front surface of the glass, and the other arrow represents the probability that light will be reflected from the back surface. Combining the arrows gives the final probability of the light being reflected. Because the glass is so thin, the additional time it took for the photon to move through it to reflect from the back surface as compared with the front surface is small, thus the direction of the stopwatch hand barely differs, resulting in a very short combined arrow. If the length of the front arrow is 0.2 and the length of the back arrow is 0.2, the calculated length of the combined arrow is 0.05, so the resulting probability of light being reflected from a thin sheet of glass is 0.0025 or 0.25 percent. The thinner the glass, the shorter the final arrow will be, and the probability of a photon being reflected approaches zero.

Conversely, as the glass increases in thickness, it will take longer for the photon to move through the glass, and the difference in the direction of the front and back stopwatch hands will increase until the difference is 180 degrees. After reversing the direction of the front stopwatch hand to create the first arrow, the effect is both arrows pointing the same direction. The final arrow would have a length of 0.4, which equals 0.16, or 16 percent, after squaring it. After that point, the two arrows will begin moving closer to one another again, until the thickness reaches the exact point where the stopwatch hand representing the direction of the back reflection reaches its original position, and the two arrows cancel each other out, giving a combined arrow with a value of zero. As the glass thickness continues to increase, the stopwatch hand circles the clock again and again, resulting in a cycling of the final probabilities between 0 and 16 percent.

One can use this approach to explain *iridescence*, the colorful arrangement reflecting from soap bubbles or oil on a mud puddle. The thin film of soap or oil acts similarly to the sheet of glass. One can use probability amplitudes to compute predictions relating to other characteristics of light, such as the fact that it travels in straight lines, it reflects at the same angle as it enters, and that a lens focuses light. In fact, every phenomenon of light can be explained by Feynman's theory of QED. Physicists calculate the probability of compound events, a succession of multiple independent events, by multiplying the final arrows for each individual event. The approach for the calculations is the same, but multiplying arrows is accomplished by shrinking and turning the arrows, that is, shortening the length of the arrows and moving the hand of the stopwatch.

How do these arrows explain the interaction of light and matter, the goal of QED? The photons of light are not really bouncing off the surface of the glass but are interacting with particles of matter, the electrons inside the glass. An electron absorbs a photon and then emits another one that subsequently is absorbed by another electron, and so on. Once thought to be only particles, Louis de Broglie demonstrated that electrons exhibit the quantum mechanical behavior of also possessing wavelike characteristics. As such, electron behavior becomes complicated as possibilities such as interference, a characteristic of waves, must be taken into account; arrows must be combined to predict all the likely positions an electron may take in spacetime.

QED states that three basic actions of photons and electrons produce all the phenomena of light and matter: a photon moves from one place to another, an electron moves from one place to another, and an electron emits or absorbs a photon. Each of these actions has its own amplitude. The probability or amplitude of a photon moving from point A in spacetime to point B in spacetime, P(A to B), is diagrammatically represented by a wavy line. The amplitude formula for the second action, an electron moving from point A in spacetime to point B in spacetime, E(A to B), also depends on the differences in location and time. Though a single straight line between two points represents the moving electron, the line is really the sum of many amplitudes, since an infinite number of possible paths exist between A and B. The third action, termed a *junction*, or coupling, occurs when two straight lines meet a wavy line and equals the value j, which

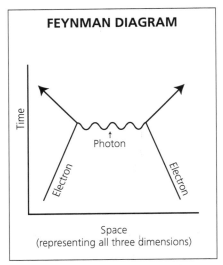

FEYNMAN DIAGRAM

Time

Photon

Electron

Electron

Space
(representing all three dimensions)

This archetypal Feynman diagram represents the interaction of two electrons.
They approach one another, exchange a
photon, and are deflected.

is approximately equal to –0.1 (a shrink to about one-tenth and a half turn). The rules of QED determine what actions occur at the junctions.

These three simple actions can be combined in various ways to represent numerous compli-cated events and to calculate the probability of an event occurring. For example, a physicist could calculate the prob-ability of two electrons moving to two different locations. Determining all the possible ways this may occur and then mul-tiplying and adding the numerous amplitudes is arduous, but using Feynman's diagrams greatly simplifies the process since wave equations can be devel-oped from the diagrams. Physicists even can use diagrams to depict events that are too complicated to calculate.

The Royal Swedish Academy of Sciences awarded Feynman, Julian Schwinger (1918–94) from Harvard University, and Shin'ichirō Tomonaga (1906–79) from Japan the Nobel Prize in physics for 1965 for their fundamental work in QED with pro-found consequences for elementary particle physics. All three simultaneously showed that the problematic infinite results of QED could be eliminated by *renormalization*, or redefining the parameters that describe the mass and charge of the electron. While Schwinger and Tomonaga accomplished this by building onto the preexisting formulas concerning electric and magnetic fields, Feynman did so by focusing on the movement of particles from place to place in spacetime and by inventing a completely new pictorial approach based on a few straightforward rules, simplifying the process immensely. As a result, physicists have been able to calculate extremely accurate values for phenomenon that have been experimentally supported.

An Intellectually Stimulating Environment

After spending a sabbatical year in Brazil from 1951 to 1952, Feynman joined the California Institute of Technology and remained there until his death, significantly contributing to a variety of topics. He examined the strange properties of liquid helium—defiance of gravity, flowing without friction, two distinct liquid phases at low temperatures, and the impossibility of freezing. In his typical manner, Feynman ignored everyone else's previous work and used his path integral approach to explain the atomic theory of *superfluidity*, the absence of any viscosity of liquid helium at near *absolute zero*. Absolute zero is the theoretical temperature at which particles have the lowest possible energy while still obeying quantum rules. (Particles need to have a tiny bit of movement or else one could determine their position and momentum simultaneously, violating Heisenberg's uncertainty principle.) From 1953 to 1958, Feynman published 10 papers explaining the quantum mechanical basis of the superfluidity of liquid helium.

From 1956 to 1957, Feynman researched the weak interaction, the interaction between elementary particles that results in the gradual radioactive decay of unstable elements. An interaction called the strong nuclear force overcomes the electrical force that repels protons from each other, tightly holding them together with neutrons in the nucleus of an atom. He believed that a much weaker nuclear force was also present and that this *weak force* instigated beta decay of radioactive elements. In beta decay, a neutron inside of an unstable nucleus spontaneously decays into a proton, emitting an electron and an *antineutrino*, a stable atomic particle that has no charge and no measurable mass. The short-range weak force is responsible for changing the nature of the particle, leading to the emission of an electron from the nucleus. Feynman's explanation for the weak interaction followed the same rules as QED; it even had the same kind of infinites that renormalization eliminated. His colleague, Murray Gell-Mann (1929–), already had arrived at the same conclusions, and at the encouragement of their department chair, Feynman and Gell-Mann jointly published their paper, "Theory of the Fermi Interaction," in *Physical Review* in 1958. This paper contributed to the *parity* revolution, when physicists realized that the long-held *symmetry* principle of parity was not universal, that the laws of nature differed depending on right- or left-handed orientation. Feynman and Gell-Mann suggested that only the left-handed part of the wave function entered into weak interactions and that the weak interaction was universal, meaning that the force had the same strength for all particles. These studies also led to the prediction that protons and neutrons must consist of even smaller entities. Many physicists believe that Feynman's work on superfluidity and on the weak interaction was worthy of another Nobel Prize.

Feynman also contributed to Gell-Mann's discovery of *quarks* and development of the theory of *quantum chromodynamics* that helps explain the internal structure of subatomic particles. He helped to elucidate the nature of the paired elementary particles called quarks by proposing the existence of what he named *partons*, small nuclear entities that interacted with electrons.

Having made significant contributions to the understanding of two of the fundamental forces of nature, electromagnetism and the weak interaction, Feynman moved on to gravitation. He wanted to develop a quantum theory of gravitation and began in the typical Feynman manner by completely developing the existing theory from scratch. He showed that classical theory could be explained in terms of interactions between particles that have mass and exchange *gravitons*, hypothetical particles that transfer gravitational forces. This approach was no more successful than Albert Einstein's in the quantum realm, however, and Feynman's research on this topic was not appreciated until the 1980s and 1990s.

When the undergraduate physics program at Caltech needed revitalization in the early 1960s, Feynman accepted the challenge to teach an introductory physics course. He was a fantastic lecturer who hardly used any formal notes and entertained the audience while clearly explaining complicated topics. His dramatic lectures became famous and were compiled into *The Feynman Lectures on Physics* (1963–65), a three-volume textbook that became a classic introduction to physics. Many of his other lectures on additional topics have been published since then.

A Public Legacy

The explosion of the space shuttle *Challenger* and death of its seven brave crew members on January 28, 1986, devastated the nation. Feynman was the only scientist on the presidential commission formed to investigate the cause of the accident, and NASA, embarrassed by his harsh conclusions, only reluctantly included his report as an appendix after much arguing. On that fateful day, engineers had warned that it was too cold to proceed with the mission, but the authorities ignored the pleas, and the shuttle exploded shortly after its launch. At a live press conference, Feynman bent a rubber O-ring with a clamp then dropped it into a glass of ice water, and the media watched it struggle to regain its shape in the cold. This dramatic demonstration showed that the slow reaction of the O-rings, due to the cold temperatures that day, allowed hot gases to escape and scorch the O-ring that was supposed to seal the joint, burning a hole in the rocket booster. The tragedy could have been prevented.

Feynman was married to Mary Louise Bell from 1952 to 1956, and he married a third time to Gweneth Howarth in 1960. Together they had one son, Carl, in 1962, and adopted a daughter, Michelle, in 1968. A decade later, Feynman was diagnosed with stomach cancer. After surgery to remove an abdominal tumor, he was given a depressing prognosis, a zero chance of surviving 10 years. The next decade brought three additional surgeries to remove reappearing cancerous masses, but he continued teaching until two weeks before his death.

After slipping into a coma, cancer claimed the life of Dick Feynman on February 15, 1988, in Los Angeles, California. His sister reported that days before he passed away, he came out of his coma briefly and said, "This dying is boring." A remarkable scientist, problem solver, and solution explainer, he belonged to many organizations, including the American Physical Society, the American Association for the Advancement of Science, the National Academy of Sciences (a membership he later resigned), and the Royal Society of London as a foreign member. In 1954, he won the Albert Einstein Award and in 1973, the Niels Bohr International Gold Medal. Two memoirs, *"Surely You're Joking, Mr. Feynman!"* and *What Do You Care What Other People Think?* reveal a more personal side of the self-described curious character, the always-grinning, pretentiousness-loathing, bongo-drumming prankster.

Feynman's legacy to physics is highlighted by his reformulation of quantum electrodynamics in which he clarified fundamental principles and simplified complex mathematical expressions by developing simple graphical interpretations to illustrate particle interactions. Of four fundamental forces in nature, Feynman's research profoundly influenced two, electromagnetism and the weak interaction, and made contributions to the third and fourth, gravitation and the strong nuclear force. His discoveries advanced particle physics and explained superfluidity. Before and after his death, many students and teachers have surpassed simple learning into comprehending physics from studying a popular three-volume collection of his captivating lectures, *The Feynman Lectures on Physics.* Just as important as his Nobel Prize–winning contributions to science are the gifts Feynman bestowed to the thousands of pupils and colleagues who interacted with him—a deeper understanding and love for a subject that he found delightful.

CHRONOLOGY

1918	Richard Feynman is born May 11th in New York, New York
1939	Graduates with a bachelor's degree in physics from MIT
1941–45	Participates in the Manhattan Project at Princeton University and at Los Alamos

1942	Earns a Ph.D. in theoretical physics from Princeton University
1945	Becomes associate professor of physics at Cornell University
1948–49	Publishes a series of papers redefining classical electrodynamics, reformulating QED, and introducing his path integral approach and famous diagrams
1950	Joins Caltech as a professor of theoretical physics
1953–58	Uses quantum mechanics to explain the superfluidity of liquid helium
1958	Publishes theory of weak interaction jointly with Murray Gell-Mann to explain beta decay
1959	Becomes the Richard Chase Tolman Professor of Physics at Caltech
1963–65	Publishes *The Feynman Lectures in Physics* in three volumes
1965	Shares the Nobel Prize in physics with Shin'ichirō Tomonaga and Julian Schwinger for their fundamental work in quantum electrodynamics (QED)
1985	Publishes *QED: The Strange Theory of Light and Matter*
1986	Serves on the Rogers Commission investigating the explosion of the space shuttle *Challenger*
1988	Dies from cancer February 15th in Los Angeles, California

FURTHER READING

Feynman, Richard P. *QED: The Strange Theory of Light and Matter.* Princeton, N.J.: Princeton University Press, 1985. Feynman's own explanation of the formidable theory of quantum electrodynamics written for the general public.

———. *"Surely You're Joking, Mr. Feynman!" Adventures of a Curious Character.* New York: W. W. Norton, 1985. Amusing bits of Feynman's life story, revealing his mischievous personality.

Gribbin, John, and Mary Gribbin. *Richard Feynman: A Life in Science.* New York: Dutton, 1997. Full-length personal biography.

Nobelprize.org. "The Nobel Prize in Physics 1965." Available online. URL: http://nobelprize.org/physics/laureates/1965. Last modified on June 16, 2000. Contains links for Feynman's biography, Nobel lecture, and other related resources.

Olson, Richard, ed. *Biographical Encyclopedia of Scientists.* Vol. 2. New York: Marshall Cavendish, 1998. Clear, concise summary of major events in the scientists' lives at an accessible level.

Murray Gell-Mann

10

(1929–   )

Murray Gell-Mann won the 1969 Nobel Prize in physics for the development of his classification scheme for elementary particles. (© *The Nobel Foundation*)

Classification of Elementary Particles and Their Interactions

Of what is the world composed? Atoms were thought to be the smallest unit of matter; the root of the word *atom* even meant indivisible. Then in 1897, Sir Joseph John Thomson discovered the first subatomic particle, the negatively charged electron. In 1911, British physicist Ernest Rutherford described the structure of the atom as a dense nucleus surrounded by orbiting electrons, and three years later he announced the existence of protons, positively charged nuclear particles. When another British physicist, Sir James Chadwick, discovered the neutron in 1932, physicists confidently believed they had identified the fundamental particles of matter, the building blocks that comprised everything in the universe. The electron, proton, and neutron were actually just leaders in a parade of hundreds of subatomic particles that were discovered by the middle of the 20th century. Perplexed scientists called the procession the "particle zoo" and searched frantically for a means to organize the hodgepodge of minute morsels. American physicist Murray Gell-Mann found the connection in an abstract mathematical model and classified elementary particles based on their symmetry properties. Gell-Mann's scheme, the *eightfold way*, led to his proposal of quarks as the ultimate building blocks of matter and to the development of quantum chromodynamics as the field theory explaining the force responsible for holding atomic nuclei together.

Pet Genius

Murray Gell-Mann was born on September 15, 1929, to Arthur Isidore and Pauline Reichstein Gell-Mann in New York, New York. Murray's father, an immigrant from Austria-Hungary, ran a language school that closed down during the Great Depression, forcing him to obtain a position as a bank custodian. The couple already had a nine-year-old son named Ben, who took Murray under his wing and introduced him to science through trips to the local museums and bike rides in the nearby park where they identified birds, trees, and insects. By age three, Murray could read and carry out multiplication in his head, and by age seven he beat 12-year-old competitors in a spelling bee. Murray enrolled in a private school on a full scholarship and quickly skipped several grades. Older students called Gell-Mann the school's "pet genius" and sometimes teased him during gym class. Graduated by the time he was 14, Murray received a full scholarship to Yale, where youthful awkwardness gradually disappeared, and he flourished academically and socially.

Murray wanted to study archaeology or linguistics, but his father encouraged him to major in something that he believed was more financially dependable, such as engineering. They agreed on physics, though Murray hated the subject in high school. At Yale, he became entranced by theoretical physics and sometimes annoyed the other students with his ability to know the answers to problems without even working through the steps. After obtaining a bachelor's degree in physics in 1948, Gell-Mann proceeded to the Massachusetts Institute of Technology (MIT) and earned a doctorate degree in physics in only three years. Victor Weisskopf, a nuclear physicist who had served as a leader of the Manhattan Project during World War II, advised Gell-Mann on his dissertation topic, events following neutron bombardment of an atomic nucleus. Learning physics and mathematics came easily to him, but writing did not. For his entire life, Gell-Mann procrastinated at writing up his ideas, and a fear of being wrong in intractable print prevented him from submitting his papers from publication in a timely manner.

J. Robert Oppenheimer, who headed the construction of the atomic bomb during World War II and was the director of the Institute for Advanced Study at Princeton, gave Gell-Mann a temporary appointment. Gell-Mann collaborated with his officemate, Francis Low, on his first scientific paper, "Bound States in Quantum Field Theory," that was published in *Physical Review* in 1951. The University of Chicago hired him as an instructor at the Institute for Nuclear Studies in 1952, and his growing reputation as a particle physicist earned him a promotion to assistant professor in 1953. After holding a visiting professorship at Columbia University for one year, the California Institute of Technology lured him away with an impressive salary offer and an associate professorship with full tenure in 1955. The following year, Gell-Mann became the youngest person to be named a full professor at the institution.

Before moving to Pasadena that summer, he married a British archeology student, J. Margaret Dow. They had a daughter named Lisa born in 1956 and a son named Nicholas born in 1963.

Classification of Elementary Particles

Until scientists discovered unstable particles in cosmic rays in the mid-20th century, they believed that the electron, proton, and neutron were the most fundamental particles of matter. Electrons were very tiny negatively charged particles that orbited around the atomic nucleus that contained the protons and the neutrons. Around the time when Gell-Mann entered academia, physicists were rapidly discovering numerous new subatomic particles—positrons in 1932, followed shortly thereafter by *muons* and *pions*. Positrons were the *antimatter* equivalent of electrons; pions and muons were similar to electrons but much heavier. The use of particle *accelerators* beginning in the 1930s eliminated the need to rely on incoming cosmic rays to collect particles for analysis. The ability to produce these particles on demand led to the rapid discovery of more than 100 kinds of subatomic particles, and every particle had its own antimatter particle with an identical mass but an opposite electrical charge or magnetic properties.

By the early 1950s, scientists faced a chaotic conglomeration that Oppenheimer called the subatomic "particle zoo." Scientists looked for patterns to organize the particles into groups, originally using mass as the primary determinant. *Leptons* were the lightest group and contained electrons, positrons, and *neutrinos*. The middleweight *mesons* included pions and kaons. *Baryons* were the heaviest and included protons and neutrons. Everyone had their own preference for how to sort the particles; Gell-Mann thought it was best to use the interactions in which the particles participated.

The different types of forces that act between particles included gravitational, electromagnetic, strong, and weak. The concept of a field described interactions between elementary particles as exchanges of other elementary particles, and quantum theory said that the exchanges must occur in discrete quantities. Gravitons are the hypothetical carriers of gravitation, the attractive interaction between all particles; however, this interaction is so weak that elementary particles physicists do not give it much consideration. Electrons emit and absorb particles called photons that carry the *electromagnetic force*, interactions that the theory of quantum elec-

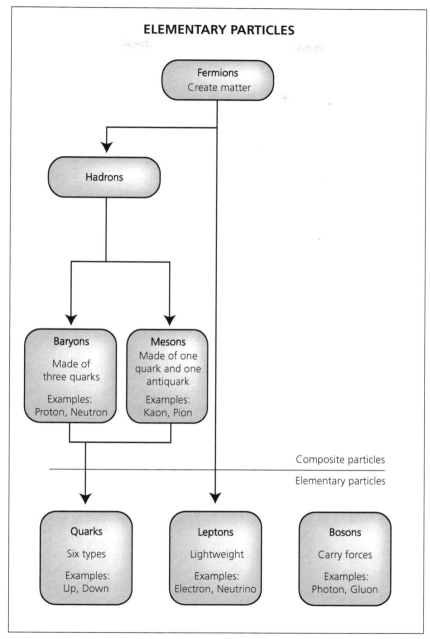

All particles are either force-carrying bosons or matter-creating fermions. Fermions are classified as leptons or hadrons that are ultimately composed of quarks.

trodynamics (QED) elegantly explained. The nature of the nuclear interactions, the strong and weak forces, was still a mystery.

Gell-Mann grouped together elementary particles that participated in the strong interactions, forming a family called the *hadrons* that was further divided according to spin, a *quantum number* that represents the angular momentum of an elementary particle. The baryons had half-unit spins, and mesons had integer units of spin. Leptons do not participate in strong interactions, but leptons and hadrons both participate in weak interactions.

Among the newest species to join the particle zoo were some unstable particles that only lived for 10^{-23} second (one over a denominator of one with 23 zeros following it) and others that remained for 10^{-10} second, longer than existing strong interaction models predicted. To explain the resistance of some particles to decay, Gell-Mann proposed the existence of a new quantum number that he called *strangeness* and concluded that, like charge, it must be conserved during a strong or electromagnetic interaction. That is, if a particle with a strangeness value of +1 decayed, the total sum of the strangeness values for the decay products must also equal one. He assigned ordinary particles, such as protons and neutrons, a strangeness of zero and *strange particles* either +1 or −1 (others discovered later had other whole number values). When *nucleons* and pions collided, strange particles formed. Since the strangeness of the ordinary parent particles had to be zero (by definition of ordinary), then the creation of a particle with a strangeness of +1 necessitated that another strangeness particle of −1 also form to conserve the total strangeness. (This production in pairs was called *associated production*.) If either of the newly created strange particles decayed back into an ordinary particle by the *strong force*, then the strangeness would not be conserved. Decay from strong force interactions occurred rapidly, while weak force interactions did not conserve strangeness and occurred more slowly, thus the particles with lifetimes longer than expected decayed by weak force interactions. This system, proposed around 1953 by Gell-Mann and independently by Kazuhiko Nishijima, predicted that some associated pairs should be produced more often than others, a prediction confirmed by Brookhaven National Laboratory accelerator experiments.

Though the strangeness theory explained prolonged decay and associated production, others initially had difficulty accepting some aspects of Gell-Mann's proposal. Within a few years, however, the strangeness quantum number had become deeply rooted. Researchers kept finding new particles that the theory predicted.

Meeting of the Minds

In Pasadena, Gell-Mann flourished with the brilliant physicist Richard Feynman as his stimulating yet exasperating theory-sparring partner and his new wife at home. He researched a problem related to the long-living particles from which he developed the concept of strangeness and the *conservation law* of symmetry, a change that leaves everything else the same. To illustrate symmetry, Feynman explained that an alarm clock acts the same no matter where or when it is; its behavior is said to be symmetrical in space and time. If taken to a different time zone, the hands move around the face of the clock at the same speed, and it will work the same next week or next year as it works today. The symmetry Gell-Mann studied was called *parity*, a quantum number related to reflection, as an object appears in a mirror image. Even in a mirror image, a clock reads the same, the arrows still point to the same numbers, and the hands still pass through number one on the way to number two; only the right and left are exchanged. Physicists long assumed that nature did not recognize right- versus left-handedness, in other words, parity was conserved, but the behavior of strange particles suggested that parity was not conserved. Gell-Mann solved this puzzle but was hesitant to publish his solution in case his idea was wrong. In early 1956, he was horrified to see a prepublication print of an article by T. D. Lee and Frank Yang proposing the same thing. The idea eventually proved false, but Gell-Mann resolved to never be scooped again.

That spring Gell-Mann attended a conference where physicists discussed the violation of parity and suggested that the weak force violated parity. Italian-born American physicist Enrico Fermi had introduced the weak force as a mediator of beta decay in 1933. In this process, a neutron transformed into a proton and emitted an electron and an antineutrino. The creation of the electron conserved charge during the reaction, and the antineutrino conserved energy and angular momentum. More than 20 years later, the nature of the weak force was still a mystery. Lee and Yang suggested experiments to determine if weak interactions conserved parity. In January 1957, researchers found convincing evidence that parity was broken during beta decay—electrons were emitted preferentially in one direction.

In quantum theory, particles were represented by waves that took on different shapes when the weak force caused decay. Gell-Mann wanted to determine which two of five possible types of transformations explained all weak interactions, including beta decay. Recent experiments suggested two types for one interaction and two different types for a second interaction, and physicists wondered if no universal weak interaction existed. After discussing the problem with E. C. George Sudarshan and Robert Marshak, who were visiting California from the University of Rochester, Gell-Mann recognized the pattern followed by weak interactions and planned on including it in another paper he was going to write, but then he found out Feynman had formulated the same conclusions. Gell-Mann was annoyed at Feynman's arrogance and did not want him to get credit for the discovery, but their department head suggested that joint authorship on a paper was in the best interest of the school. "Theory of the Fermi Interaction," published in *Physical Review* in 1958, brought praise to both Feynman and Gell-Mann, and though they acknowledged Sudarshan and Marshak, history mostly credits the Caltech professors.

Quantum field theory did not seem to explain the nuclear interactions as elegantly as it described electromagnetism. Infinites plagued equations for nuclear interactions, even after Gell-Mann and Feynman developed their theory of the weak force. Physicists believed pions carried the strong force and had no idea what carried the weak force. The problem with pions as strong force carriers was they had to be massive to explain the very short interaction range, but the field had to extend everywhere, so it had to travel the speed of light, which meant it had to be carried by massless *bosons*.

In a weak interaction, two particles entered with one set of quantum numbers and came out with another set. Gell-Mann suggested "uxyls," also referred to as X particles, as the bosons for the weak force. At least two were needed to carry away scraps of charge when a weak interaction changed the charge of a particle (as when a neutron decayed into a proton in beta decay), and Gell-Mann suspected two additional neutral particles existed. He thought *unification* of the weak force with electromagnetism might help solve the problem, but was quantum field theory the right framework? And why was strangeness sometimes conserved and sometimes not?

Eightfold Way

Frustrated, Gell-Mann switched his focus to the strong force, and he started looking for patterns in hadrons, the group of particles that felt the strong force. A Caltech mathematician working on group theory reminded Gell-Mann about a grouping system based on symmetry. Realizing this may be the key to uniting the hadrons, he started arranging the particles by strangeness and electric charge into higher orders. When everything finally came together, he found a pattern complete with eight baryons and a similar pattern with seven mesons. In 1961, Gell-Mann described an abstract mathematical method that he named the eightfold way for arranging hadrons into families based on properties of symmetry. Israeli physicist Yuval Ne'eman independently proposed the same method. What appeared to be several separate particles was simply a single particle with different configurations for its quantum numbers. Baryons with similar spin and parity comprised one group, and mesons with identical spin and parity belonged to another. The scheme suggested that heavier baryons should form a group of 10 members. Nine of these 10 particles were identified already.

Every field was described by one of these groups: group U(1) for electromagnetism, SU(2) for *isospin* symmetry (isospin is the quantum number used to differentiate opposite manifestations of the same particle), and SU(3) for the eightfold way. When Gell-Mann devised this classification scheme, he predicted the existence and

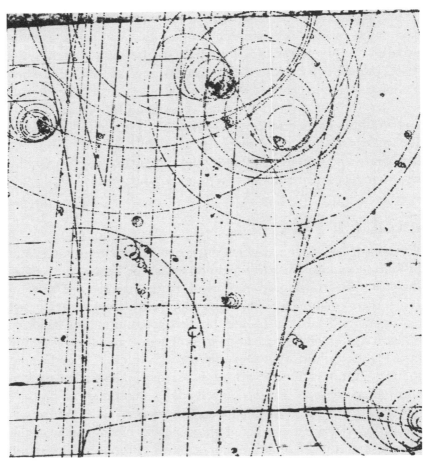

This historic photograph of particle tracks from a device used to detect
particles created by an accelerator provided evidence for the existence of the
omega-minus particle that Gell-Mann predicted by the eightfold way.
(Brookhaven National Laboratory/Photo Researchers, Inc.)

properties of several undiscovered particles, including the baryon
omega-minus to complete the group of 10 heavy hadrons. A newly
discovered eighth meson had properties that fit it into a pattern
similar to the eightfold baryon pattern. Experiments conducted in
1963 at Brookhaven National Laboratory produced an omega-
minus particle, confirming the eightfold way.

Proposal of Quarks

The symmetry patterns of the eightfold way suggested that hadrons consisted of a set of similar particles. In 1964, Gell-Mann published a short paper in *Physical Letters*, "A Schematic Model of Baryons and Mesons," proposing that subatomic particles he named quarks were the stable, smallest, building blocks of all matter, tremendously simplifying the field of elementary particle physics. At the same time, a former graduate student of Gell-Mann and Feynman, George Zweig from CERN, arrived at the same hypothesis. Quarks were unusual because their assigned electric charges were only a fraction of the proton charge. He initially described three "flavors" of quarks (u for up with a fractional electric charge of +2/3, d for down with a charge of −1/3, and s for strange with a charge of −1/3) and was able to describe the composition of the hundreds of subatomic particles from these three building blocks. Though Gell-Mann was a theoretical physicist, experiments performed by others substantiated his quark theory. When experiments suggested the three-quark model was no longer sufficient to explain everything, physicists proposed a fourth (c for *charm* with a charge of +2/3). Later, when additional larger leptons were discovered, top (t, charge of +2/3) and bottom (b, charge of −1/3) charms were also predicted, bringing the total number of leptons and quarks to six each.

A proton consisted of two up quarks and one down quark, (+2/3) + (+2/3) + (−1/3), giving it a total electrical charge of +1, and the fact that it had more ups than downs gave it an up isospin. One up and two down quarks created an electrically neutral neutron, (+2/3) + (−1/3) + (−1/3) = 0, and because it had more downs than ups, it had a down isospin. When particles decayed, the weak force changed the value of one quark; when a neutron (ddu) decayed into a proton (duu), one down quark changed into an up quark.

The quark theory seemed to work, but were the quarks real or contrived mathematical entities? No other particle was known to possess fractional charges, and experimenters were unsuccessful in tracking down quarks in cosmic rays, accelerators, or anywhere else. In 1968, physicists began to accumulate evidence of electrons

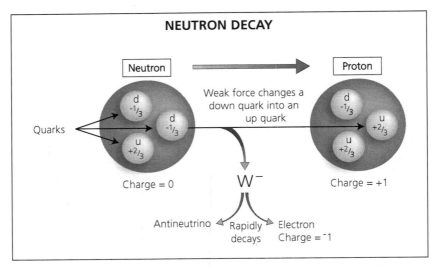

NEUTRON DECAY

Neutron → Proton

Quarks

Neutron: d $-\frac{1}{3}$, d $-\frac{1}{3}$, u $+\frac{2}{3}$

Weak force changes a down quark into an up quark

Proton: d $-\frac{1}{3}$, u $+\frac{2}{3}$, u $+\frac{2}{3}$

Charge = 0

W⁻

Charge = +1

Antineutrino — Rapidly decays — Electron Charge = ⁻1

Weak forces transform a neutron into a proton, emitting a W⁻ particle that rapidly decays into an electron and an antineutrino.

hitting and bouncing off something inside a proton, but quarks cannot be separated from their triads and therefore can never be directly observed.

Gell-Mann received the Nobel Prize in physics for 1969 for his contributions and discoveries concerning the classification of elementary particles and their interactions. Though he shared credit with his codiscoverers of strangeness, the eightfold way, and quarks (Nishijima, Ne'eman, and Zweig, respectively), this award belonged to Gell-Mann alone. After impressing the Swedes by speaking in their native language for part of his Nobel acceptance speech, he procrastinated in submitting his lecture to the celebratory publication *Le Prix Nobel*, and despite numerous requests, he never sent one.

Quantum Chromodynamics

Others accepted Gell-Mann's field theory of the strong force involving quarks and bosons long before he was convinced it was more than a mathematical contrivance. By 1995, particle physicists had obtained experimental evidence for all six quarks, which as it turned out, not only came in flavors, but in three *"colors."* The addition of this quantum number was necessary to respect Pauli's exclusion principle. Colored particles (quarks) attracted one another by exchanging *gluons*, carriers of the strong force (also called the color force), just as electrons interacted by exchanging photons, carriers of the electromagnetic force. This exchange of gluons between quarks from different protons held them together tightly even though their electrical charges simultaneously pushed them apart. Whereas individual quarks carried the color charge, hadrons and mesons did not. Hadrons contained three quarks of three different colors: red, blue, and green. Combined, these colors cancelled each other out, just as these primary colors of visible light combined to form white light. Mesons were composed of one quark and one antiquark, so if the quark was red, the anti-red antiquark eliminated the color charge in the meson. Color conservation prevented combinations other than pairs of a color and its anticolor or triplets of all three colors.

One aspect of the strong force theory that continued to puzzle Gell-Mann and others was that individual quarks were never observed. In 1973, the presentation of a concept called *asymptotic freedom* explained this puzzle, stating that the force holding the quarks together intensified at longer distances, just the opposite as with electromagnetism or gravity. In 2004, David J. Gross, H. David Politzer, and Frank Wilczek shared the Nobel Prize in physics for the discovery of asymptotic freedom in the theory of the strong interaction.

The property of asymptotic freedom completed the theory called quantum chromodynamics (QCD). Hadrons were composed of quarks that were held together by a color force, a field carried by eight different massless bosons called "gluons" that differed only in their color properties. The color charge mediated the strong interactions between quarks and antiquarks. QCD explained how strong forces held atomic particles together so tightly, and the quark scheme explained all the possible interactions between nuclear particles and the similar symmetries within groups. Many brilliant minds contributed to the development of all the elements of QCD, and Gell-Mann's fingerprints covered many of the pieces.

Striving Toward Unification

Quarks are the fundamental building blocks of all subatomic particles; they are the simplest form of matter, and they might eventually theoretically unify all the natural forces. Physicists have attempted to develop a unified field theory that will explain everything from the interactions of subatomic particles to the revolution of the planets around the Sun. In the 1960s, physicists proposed a unified theory of the electromagnetic and weak interactions that involved the exchange of four particles: the photon, W^+, W^-, and Z^0. During the 1970s, physicists related the strong and *electroweak forces* in what is called the *standard model,* a description of all the particles and forces with the exception of gravity. The standard model is the only mathematical description that incorporates the theory of relativity and quantum mechanics.

All particles are either *fermions,* which make up matter, or bosons, which transmit forces between particles of matter. The fermions are grouped into three families or generations of four elementary particles each, with the major difference between families being size. Each family has two leptons, a negatively charged particle that interacts with an electromagnetic field and an associated, neutral neutrino. The remaining two particles in each family are quarks, the fundamental building blocks for the hadrons, the particles that have strong interactions. Quarks are characterized by two properties, flavor and color, and each family contains its own pair of flavors. The pairing of leptons and quarks within each interaction is called lepton-quark symmetry, but the underlying connection is unknown.

Quarks carry fractional electric charges. Relative to the −1 charge of an electron, the up, charm, and top quarks have a charge of +2/3, whereas the down, strange, and bottom quarks have a charge of −1/3. Because they carry charges, quarks participate in electromagnetic and weak interactions. As the building blocks of hadrons, quarks also experience strong interactions, mediated by gluons that hold the hadrons together. Each quark can come in three colors, with which the gluons interact. Since leptons do not have color, they do not feel strong interactions, but gluons, of which there are eight types, do have color. A unique feature of gluon interaction is that the strength increases as the distance increases, meaning if something tries to pull quarks apart, the result is a tighter bond. Because of this, individual quarks or gluons have never been observed, but overwhelming evidence supports their existence. Hadrons, composed of colored quarks, do not exhibit color, because the colors cancel each other out. QCD is the theory that describes the strong force carried by gluons.

Efforts to develop a quantum field theory for gravitational interactions have been unsuccessful. String theory describes particles as extended two-dimensional objects rather than point-like particles. Superstring theory, involving 10 dimensions, could be fundamental in developing a *grand unified theory* for all four forces during this century.

THE STANDARD MODEL

Interactions

Boson	Force	Participating Fermions
Photon	Electromagnetism	All charged particles
W^+, W^-, Z^0	Weak	Hadrons and leptons
Eight different gluons	Strong/Color	Hadrons
Graviton	Gravitation	Everything

Families

	First generation	Second generation	Third generation
Leptons	Electron Electron-neutrino	Muon Muon-neutrino	Tau Tau-neutrino
Quarks	Up Down	Charm Strangeness	Top Bottom
Found in	Ordinary matter	Cosmic rays or accelerator experiments	

The standard model describes quarks, leptons, and force-carrying particles.

A Busy Retirement

Following his Nobel Prize, many distractions kept Gell-Mann on the fringes of physics; in particular, his wife Margaret died of cancer in 1981 and, in 1992, he married a poet and English professor, Marcia Southwick. He served as a regent of the Smithsonian Institution (1974–88) and as director of the MacArthur Foundation (1979–2002). Gell-Mann has appreciated nature since his days of bird-watching in the park with his older brother, and in 1993 he received the Lindbergh Award for his efforts in promoting balance between advancing technology and conservation. In 1984, Gell-Mann helped found the Santa Fe Institute, a research and education center where theorists collaborate on topics ranging from quantum mechanics to economics to understand better the simple mechanisms underlying complex interactions. Having retired from Caltech in 1993, he currently serves on the board of trustees for the Santa Fe Institute and has served as chairman of the board (1984–85) and cochair of the science board (1985–2000). He has written books about the topic of complexity for a popular audience: *The Quark and the Jaguar* (1994) and *The Regular and the Random* (2005). Living in Santa Fe, he still enjoys linguistics, ornithology, and archeology. He teaches part-time at the University of New Mexico and continues to feed his hunger for patterns by researching the basis of complex phenomena.

Gell-Mann belongs to the American Physical Society, which awarded him the Dannie Heineman Prize for mathematical physics in 1959, and the National Academy of Sciences, which awarded him the John J. Carty Medal in 1968. He also belongs to the Royal Society of London as a foreign member and the American Academy of Arts and Sciences, and he has received awards from the Franklin Institute and the Atomic Energy Commission. At least one dozen academic institutions have awarded Gell-Mann honorary doctorate degrees.

Gell-Mann's proposal of the eightfold way provided theoretical physicists a framework for classifying the plethora of subatomic particles discovered during the 20th century. His ability to recognize relationships among fundamental particles and the forces that bind them led to a better understanding of the structure of matter.

Strangeness, the eightfold way, and quarks, three of Gell-Mann's most influential ideas, all contributed to the development of the standard model that combines the electroweak and strong forces to describe particles and their interactions. This may lead to final resolution in the form of an all-encompassing grand unified theory during the 21st century.

CHRONOLOGY

1929	Murray Gell-Mann is born September 15th in New York, New York
1948	Obtains a bachelor of science degree in physics from Yale University
1951	Earns a doctorate degree in physics from MIT and joins the Institute for Advanced Study in Princeton, New Jersey
1952	Becomes an instructor at the Institute for Nuclear Studies at the University of Chicago
1953	Becomes an assistant professor of physics at the University of Chicago and proposes the property of strangeness
1954	Is promoted to associate professor at the University of Chicago and is visiting professor at Columbia University
1955	Becomes associate professor of physics at Caltech and begins studying weak interactions
1956	Becomes youngest full professor at Caltech
1958	Publishes joint paper on the theory of the weak interaction to explain beta decay with Richard Feynman
1961	Proposes the eightfold way for organizing elementary particles based on symmetries
1964	Announces that hadrons consist of fundamental particles named quarks
1967	Is named the Robert Andrews Millikan Professor of Theoretical Physics at Caltech

1969	Receives the Nobel Prize in physics for his contributions and discoveries concerning the classification of elementary particles and their interactions
1972	Presents theory of quantum chromodynamics
1984	Cofounds the Santa Fe Institute
1993	Becomes professor emeritus at Caltech and professor and distinguished fellow at the Santa Fe Institute
1994	Publishes *The Quark and the Jaguar,* exploring the origin of complexity
2005	Publishes *The Regular and the Random*

FURTHER READING

Gell-Mann, Murray. *The Quark and the Jaguar: Adventures in the Simple and the Complex.* New York: W. H. Freeman, 1994. Gell-Mann's attempt to unify basic natural laws with the complexity of the natural world.

Johnson, George. *Strange Beauty: Murray Gell-Mann and the Revolution in Twentieth-Century Physics.* New York: Alfred A. Knopf, 1999. Full-length, standard biography written for adults.

Murray Gell-Mann home page. Santa Fe Institute. Available online. URL: http://www.santafe.edu/~mgm. Accessed on January 31, 2005. Gell-Mann's Web page containing a brief biography, his curriculum vita, and a listing of his publications.

Nobelprize.org. "The Nobel Prize in Physics 1969." Available online. URL: http://nobelprize.org/physics/laureates/1969. Last modified on June 16, 2000. Contains links to the presentation speech, a brief biography, Gell-Mann's banquet speech, and other resources.

Olson, Richard, ed. *Biographical Encyclopedia of Scientists.* Vol. 2. New York: Marshall Cavendish, 1998. Clear, concise summary of major events in the scientists' lives at an accessible level.

GLOSSARY

absolute temperature   a temperature expressed as degrees above absolute zero

absolute zero   the temperature at which substances have no heat and all the molecules are motionless, theoretically equal to −459.67°F (−273.15°C)

acceleration   the rate of change of velocity

accelerator   a machine that accelerates particles to very high speeds, then crashes them into one another

alchemy   the study of how to convert ordinary metals into gold; precursor to chemistry

alpha particle   a positively charged particle that contains two protons and two neutrons; released during radioactive disintegration

amplitude   the distance between the undisturbed position of a medium and the highest point of a wave; in QED, the probability that an event will occur

antimatter   the counterpart of ordinary matter that is identical in all respects except for electrical charge, which is reversed

antineutrino   the antimatter equivalent of a neutrino

apothecary   an early pharmacist, involved in mixing and preparing drugs and herbal remedies

associated production   the creation of particles in pairs, allowing them to resist rapid disintegration by the strong force

astronomy   the scientific study of the heavenly bodies, particularly their movements, positions, composition, and distribution

asymptotic freedom   the property that results in a weaker interaction between quarks as they approach one another and a stronger interaction as their distance increases

atom   smallest bit of an element that retains all the properties of that element

atomic number   the number of protons in the nucleus of an element

atomic weight   the average weight of the naturally occurring isotopes of an element relative to carbon-12

baryon   a heavy particle that feels the strong force and is composed of three quarks

beta decay   a process in which a neutron disintegrates into a proton, a neutron, and an antineutrino

beta particle   an electron or positron released from the nucleus of an atom during radioactive disintegration

binomial theorem   a shortcut for multiplying an equation with two variables by itself many times over; $(a + b)^n$

blackbody   a body that absorbs all the radiation falling on it and also acts as a perfect radiator

bosons   particles that carry forces and have whole number values for spin

calculus   the branch of mathematics that allows continuously varying quantities to be manipulated

cathode ray   supposed agent of the fluorescence of the glass of an evacuated discharge tube; later realized to be a stream of electrons

charm   one of the six flavors of quarks, has an electrical charge of +2/3

classical physics   physics that includes the branches that were well-developed before the 20th century, including mechanics, sound, light, heat, electricity, and magnetism

color   in QCD, a hypothetical property of quarks through which the strong force acts. Includes three varieties: red, blue, and green

complementarity   physical principle proposed by Niels Bohr stating that certain concepts are complementary, meaning that an experiment that clearly illustrates one will obscure the other

compound   substance made up of two or more elements

conductor   substance through which electricity easily passes

conservation law   in particle physics, a symmetry in which a quantity remains unchanged following an interaction

correspondence   physical principle proposed by Niels Bohr stating that the predictions of quantum theory must correspond to the results of classical physics analysis

cosmic rays   very short wavelength, high-energy rays that reach the Earth's atmosphere from outer space

crest   highest point or peak of a wave

crystal   a solid composed of atoms or molecules arranged in a regular array with measurable distances between them

cyclotron   an instrument that accelerates electrically charged atomic particles using an electromagnetic field

decay series   a characteristic succession of unstable elements produced when one radioactive element decays into another until a stable end product is achieved

diamagnetism   the quality of being repelled by a magnet; taking a position at right angles to the force lines of a magnet

diffraction   the spreading out of waves as they move by an obstacle or through an opening

eightfold way   a scheme for organizing baryons and mesons into families based on symmetries, proposed independently by Murray Gell-Mann and Yuval Ne'eman

electrical induction   creation of an electric current by movement in a magnetic field; also called electromagnetic induction

electricity   a naturally occurring form of energy that can be produced by friction, a chemical reaction, or mechanical effort

electrochemistry   the branch of science relating chemistry and electricity

electrode   point at which an electric current moves from one medium to another

electrolysis   process that uses electricity to break down a compound into its elements

electromagnetic force   the long-range force that arises from electricity and magnetism

electromagnetic induction   process that uses a changing magnetic field to produce an electric current; also called electrical induction

electromagnetism magnetism developed from a current of electricity, or the branch of physics concerned with electricity and magnetism

electron a negatively charged, lightweight subatomic particle that orbits the nucleus of an atom

electron theory of metals theory stating that the motion of electrons in metals accounts for their properties

electroweak force a force that unifies the electromagnetic and the weak forces

element substance made up of only one type of atom

elliptical shaped like a large oval

emission spectrum characteristic pattern of light and color given off by an element's atoms as they release energy

energy the capacity for doing work. Comes in different forms such as light and heat

entropy the degree of disorder in a system

exclusion principle the principle stating that no two electrons of an atom can have the same quantum numbers; proposed by Wolfgang Pauli

fermions particles that comprise matter and whose spin is measured in half units

field theory any theory or the study of any theory about phenomena that occur over space or distance

force an influence that is capable of changing a body's state of rest or uniform motion in a straight line

frequency the number of times an event recurs in a given unit of time

friction a force that resists movement of one surface against another with which it is in contact

galvanometer instrument that measures electric currents

generator machine that converts mechanical energy into electrical energy; also called a dynamo

gluons carriers of the strong force that hold quarks together to form hadrons and bind nucleons to form atomic nuclei

grand unified theory a theory that unifies the strong force and the electroweak force

gravitation   the natural force of attraction between objects that acts proportional to their masses; gravity

graviton   a theoretical particle that carries the gravitational force

hadrons   group of particles that feel the strong force. Includes baryons and mesons, composed of quarks

half-life   the length of time it takes for half the amount of a radioactive substance to decay

heat   a form of energy caused by the motion of molecules

inertia   natural law stating that an object in motion remains in motion at a constant speed in a straight line, and an object at rest remains at rest unless acted upon by an outside force

infinite   boundless or endless, beyond any assignable quantity or magnitude

interference   the effect of the meeting of two waves; considered constructive if the waves reinforce one another resulting in increased amplitude and considered destructive if the amplitude is decreased

ion   an atom or molecule with a net electric charge

ionization   the process of creating ions

iridescence   a rainbowlike display of changing colors

isospin   a quantum number related to the number of different charges in a group of closely related particles

isotope   one of several atoms with the same atomic number but different atomic weights. Isotopes of an element contain the same number of protons and have similar chemical properties but contain different numbers of neutrons

junction (also **coupling**)   in a Feynman diagram, the intersection between two straight lines and a wavy line

leptons   light particles that do not feel the strong force

light   a form of radiant energy consisting of electromagnetic waves that travel at a speed of 186,282 miles (300,000 km) per second

magnetic field   area around a magnet in which its magnetism operates

magnetism   the attractive force that electric currents exert on other electric currents

mass   the amount of material in an object

matter something solid, the substance of which something is made

meson middleweight particles that feel the strong force; type of hadron made from one quark and one antiquark

modern physics physics that deals with the behaviors of matter and energy on the atomic level. Two main theories include quantum theory and relativity, both developed in the 20th century

molecules the smallest particle into which a substance (an element or a compound) can be divided and still retain its properties; consisting of two or more atoms

momentum the measure of the motion of an object, equal to its mass times its velocity

muon a type of particle that is similar to but heavier than an electron, also called mu-meson

neutrino a stable atomic particle that has no charge and no measurable mass

neutron a neutral subatomic particle with a weight similar to that of a proton; found in the nucleus of an atom

nuclear energy energy that is released when mass is transformed into energy, such as when atoms undergo nuclear fission

nuclear fission the splitting of a nucleus into two parts, resulting in the release of energy

nucleons components of an atomic nucleus; protons and neutrons

nucleus positively charged center of an atom

omega-minus a particle that Murray Gell-Mann predicted by the eightfold way

optics the scientific study of light and vision

orbit the curved course of a planet or satellite around another body

parity in quantum mechanics, the behavior of a wave function when it is reflected to form its mirror image. If the sign of the function remains unchanged, parity is even, and if the sign is changed, parity is odd

partons particles that make up hadrons, proposed by Richard Feynman

photoelectric effect the ejection of electrons from the surface of a metal plate when light particles with enough energy fall on it

photon a quantum of light energy; particle that carries the electromagnetic force

pions particles that physicists originally thought carried the strong force; also called pi-mesons

Planck's constant a constant represented by h that was introduced by Max Planck in his quantum theory and that appears in every formula of quantum mechanics

polarized light light whose waves all travel in the same direction

positron a particle with the same mass as an electron but with a positive charge

prism in optics, a triangular block of glass or plastic used to disperse light or to change its direction

proton a positively charged subatomic particle found in the nucleus of an atom

quantum (plural **quanta**) small packet of energy

quantum chromodynamics (QCD) the study of the action of forces by which the property of color binds quarks together

quantum electrodynamics (QED) the study of the electromagnetic interactions between particles of light and matter, such as photons and electrons

quantum mechanics the branch of physics that describes the structure and behavior of matter

quantum numbers numbers that represent the values for the physical properties of a particle, such as charge, mass, and spin

quarks the truly fundamental building blocks of matter that come in six "flavors" and three "colors." Quarks combine to form hadrons

radiation energy in the form of moving subatomic particles or waves

radioactivity spontaneous nuclear decay resulting in the release of alpha particles, beta particles, or gamma rays

reflection the return of a wave of energy, such as light

refraction the process of bending a ray of light as it passes at an angle from one medium to another

relativity one of two theories proposed by Albert Einstein that govern time, space, mass, motion, and gravity. The special theory of relativity states that mass and energy are equivalent and predicts changes in mass, dimension, and time that are noticeable when approaching the speed of light. The general theory of relativity deals with the equivalence of gravitational and inertial forces

renormalization   a mathematical method for eliminating infinite quantities that appear from quantum field equations

spectroscopy   the study of the spectrum

spectrum   the band of colors formed when radiant energy is broken up

spin   a quantum number representing the angular momentum of an elementary particle

standard model   the quantum field theory that relates the electroweak force with the strong force but does not unify them

strangeness   a quantum number that was invented to explain the long lifetimes of strange particles

strange particles   particles that do not decay by the strong force

strong force   the short-range force carried by gluons that binds quarks together to form hadrons and holds nucleons together

superfluidity   the frictionless flow of liquid helium at temperatures approaching absolute zero

symmetry   something that remains constant while something else changes

thermodynamics   the physics of the relationships between heat and other forms of energy

transformer   device for changing the strength or form of an electric current

transuranics   the name given by Enrico Fermi for elements produced from uranium when it is bombarded by neutrons. Experimentation showed them to be barium isotopes

trough   lowest point of a wave

uncertainty principle   principle stating that certain pairs of quantities, such as the position and velocity of a particle, cannot be measured simultaneously with accuracy, proposed by Werner Karl Heisenberg

unification   the mathematical process of showing that two phenomena are simply different manifestations of the same thing

velocity   the rate of motion

voltaic pile   an early form of an electric battery consisting of stacks of copper and zinc discs and layers of cloth or paper soaked in salt water, with a wire extending from the top to the bottom of the stack; a galvanic pile

wave   classically, a disturbance of a medium that carries energy from one place to another

wavelength   the distance between one peak or crest of a wave and the next

weak force   the short-range force that causes radioactive decay; carried by W and Z particles

W particles   positively and negatively charged particles (bosons) that carry the weak force

X-ray   an electromagnetic disturbance like light but with a much higher frequency

Z particles   neutral particles that carry the weak force

FURTHER RESOURCES

Books

Adams, Steve. *Frontiers: Twentieth-Century Physics*. New York: Taylor and Francis, 2000. A survey of 20th-century physics written for high school students.

Breithaupt, Jim. *Teach Yourself Physics*. Chicago, Ill.: NTC/Contemporary Publishing, 2002. A compact introduction to the key concepts, major discoveries, and current challenges in physics.

Bromley, D. Allan. *A Century of Physics*. New York: Springer, 2002. A tour from the last century of physics growth, impact, and directions. Numerous photos and illustrations.

Chapple, Michael. *Schaum's A to Z Physics*. New York: McGraw-Hill, 2003. Defines 650 key concepts with diagrams and graphs. Intended for high school students and college freshmen.

Charap, John M. *Explaining the Universe: The New Age of Physics*. Princeton, N.J.: Princeton University Press, 2002. A description of the field of physics at the beginning of the 21st century.

Dennis, Johnnie T. *The Complete Idiot's Guide to Physics*. Indianapolis, Ind.: Alpha Books, 2003. A friendly review of high school–level classical physics.

The Diagram Group. *The Facts On File Physics Handbook*. New York: Facts On File, 2000. Convenient resource containing a glossary of terms, short biographical profiles of celebrated physicists, a chronology of events and discoveries, and useful charts, tables, and diagrams.

Falk, Dan. *Universe on a T-Shirt: The Quest for the Theory of Everything.* New York: Arcade Publishing, 2002. A story outlining developments in the search for the theory that will unify all four natural forces.

Fleisher, Paul. *Relativity and Quantum Mechanics: Principles of Modern Physics.* Minneapolis, Minn.: Lerner Publications, 2002. An introduction to the concepts of relativity and quantum mechanics written for middle school students.

Griffith, W. Thomas. *The Physics of Everyday Phenomena.* 4th ed. Boston: WCB/McGraw-Hill, 2004. A conceptual text for nonscience college students.

Gundersen, P. Erik. *The Handy Physics Answer Book.* Detroit, Mich.: Visible Ink Press, 1999. Answers numerous questions about physics using a conceptual approach.

Holton, Gerald James, and Stephen G. Brush. *Physics, the Human Adventure: From Copernicus to Einstein and Beyond.* New Brunswick, N.J.: Rutgers University Press, 2001. Comprehensive introduction intended for nonscience college students. Difficult reading but covers a lot of material.

James, Ioan. *Remarkable Physicists: From Galileo to Yukawa.* New York: Cambridge University Press, 2004. Contains brief biographies of 50 physicists spanning a period of 250 years, focusing on the lives rather than the science.

Leiter, Darryl J. *A to Z of Physicists.* New York: Facts On File, 2003. Profiles over 150 physicists, discussing their research and contributions. Includes bibliography, cross-references, and chronology.

McGrath, Kimberley A., ed. *World of Physics.* Farmington Hills, Mich.: Thomson Gale, 2001. Contains 1,000 entries on concepts, theories, discoveries, pioneers, and issues related to physics.

Rosen, Joe. *Encyclopedia of Physics.* New York: Facts On File, 2004. Comprehensive one-volume overview containing more than 600 entries and 11 prose essays on different current topics.

Trefil, James. *From Atoms to Quarks: An Introduction to the Strange World of Particle Physics.* Rev. ed. New York: Anchor Books, 1994. A primer on this complex subject written for general readers.

Internet Resources

The ABCs of Nuclear Science. Nuclear Science Division, Lawrence Berkeley National Laboratory. Available online. URL: http://www.lbl.gov/abc. Last updated on November 18, 2004. Introduces the basics of nuclear science: nuclear structure, radioactivity, cosmic rays, antimatter, and more.

Andersen, Joseph. "Physics," Available online. URL: http://physics.about.com. Accessed on January 31, 2005. Contains regular feature articles. Visit links under "Essentials" to find a physics glossary, FAQs, constants, and formulas and links under "Articles and Resources" for topic-specific information.

Center for History of Physics. American Institute of Physics. Available online. URL: http://www.aip.org/history. Accessed on January 31, 2005. Visit the "Exhibit Hall" to learn about events such as the discovery of the electron or read selected papers of great American physicists.

A Century of Physics. American Physical Society. Available online. URL: http://timeline.aps.org. Accessed on January 31, 2005. Wonderful, interactive timeline describing major events in the development of modern physics.

Contributions of 20th Century Women to Physics. CWP and Regents of the University of California. Available online. URL: http://www.physics.ucla.edu. Accessed on January 31, 2005. Highlights 83 women who have made original and important contributions to physics.

Exploring Gravity. Curtain University of Technology. Available online. URL: http://www.curtin.edu.au/curtin/dept/phys-sci/gravity/index2.htm. Accessed on January 31, 2005. A tutorial including historical information about gravitation at three different learning levels.

Fear of Physics. Available online. URL: http://www.fearof physics.com. Accessed on January 31, 2005. Entertaining way to review physics concepts.

The Particle Adventure: The Fundamentals of Matter and Force. The Particle Data Group of the Lawrence Berkeley National

Laboratory. Available online. URL: http://www.particle adventure.org. Accessed on January 31, 2005. Interactive tour of quarks, neutrinos, antimatter, extra dimensions, dark matter, accelerators, and particle detectors.

Physics Central. American Physical Society. Available online. URL: http://www.physicscentral.com. Accessed on January 31, 2005. Updated daily with information on physics in the news, current research, and people in physics.

Physics 2000. University of Colorado at Boulder. Available online. URL: http://www.colorado.edu/physics/2000/index.pl. Accessed on January 31, 2005. A fun, interactive journey through modern physics.

StudyWorks Online! The Physics Classroom: A High School Physics Tutorial. Available online. URL: http://www.physics classroom.com. Accessed on January 31, 2005. Reviews basic physics topics and contains animations demonstrating physical concepts and a help section to practice skills.

Succeed in Physical Science. Available online. URL: http://www. school-for-champions.com/science.htm. Accessed on January 31, 2005. Lessons in a variety of physics and chemistry topics.

Windows to the Universe. "Fundamental Physics." Available online. URL: http://www.windows.ucar.edu/tour/link=/physical_ science/physics/physics.html. Last modified on March 18, 2004. Still under construction, this site will contain a broad overview of physics and already has many links to physics topics, including mechanics, electricity and magnetism, thermal physics, and atomic and particle physics.

Periodicals

Discover

Published by Buena Vista Magazines
114 Fifth Avenue
New York, NY 10011
Telephone: (212) 633-4400
www.discover.com

A popular monthly magazine containing easy to understand articles on a variety of scientific topics.

Nature

The Macmillan Building
4 Crinan Street
London N1 9XW
Telephone: +44 (0)20 7833 4000
www.nature.com/nature
A prestigious primary source of scientific literature.

Physics Today

Published by the American Institute of Physics (AIP)
Circulation and Fulfillment Division
Suite 1NO1
2 Huntington Quadrangle
Melville, NY 11747
Telephone: (516) 576-2270
www.physicstoday.org
Monthly flagship publication of AIP.

Science

Published by the American Association for the Advancement of
    Science
1200 New York Avenue NW
Washington, DC 20005
Telephone: (202) 326-6417
www.sciencemag.org
One of the most highly regarded primary sources of scientific research.

Scientific American

415 Madison Avenue
New York, NY 10017
Telephone: (212) 754-0550
www.sciam.com

A popular monthly magazine that publishes articles on a broad range of subjects and current issues in science and technology.

Societies and Organizations

American Association for the Advancement of Science (www.aaas.org) 1200 New York Avenue NW, Washington, DC 20005. Telephone: (202) 326-6400

American Physical Society (www.aps.org) One Physics Ellipse, College Park, MD 20740-3844. Telephone: (301) 209-3200

Society of Physics Students (www.spsnational.org) American Institute of Physics, One Physics Ellipse, College Park, MD 20740-3843. Telephone: (301) 209-3007